SPEECH ACT PHENOMENOLOGY

SPEECH ACT PHENOMENOLOGY

by

RICHARD L. LANIGAN

MARTINUS NIJHOFF - THE HAGUE - 1977

To my parents

TABLE OF CONTENTS

PREFACE

The nature and function of language as Man's chief vehicle of communication occupies a focal position in the human sciences, particularly in philosophy. The concept of 'communication' is problematic because it suggests both 'meaning' (the nature of language) and the activity of speaking (the function of language). The philosophic theory of 'speech acts' is one attempt to clarify the ambiguities of 'speech' as both the use of language to describe states of affair and the process in which that description is generated as 'communication'.

The present study, *Speech Act Phenomenology*, is in part an examination of speech act theory. The theory offers an explanation for speech performance, that is, the structure of speech acts as 'relationships' and the content of speech acts as 'meaning'. The primary statement of the speech act theory that is examined is that presented by Austin. A secondary concern is the formulation of the theory as presented by Searle and Grice. The limitations of the speech act theory are specified by applying the theory as an explanation of 'human communication'. This conceptual examination of 'communication' suggests that the philosophic method of 'analysis' does not resolve the antinomy of language 'nature' and 'function'. Basically, the conceptual distinctions of the speech act theory (i.e. locutions, illocutions, and perlocutions) are found to be empty as a comprehensive explanation of the concept 'communication'.

In consequence, the limitations discovered in the 'analytic' approach to the study of speech acts forms a justification for a phenomenological approach to specify the concept 'communication'. The phenomenology of speech acts presented in the present study is a phenomenological 'description', 'reduction,' and 'interpretation' of 'communication'. The description is an account of 'perception' as the communicative elements of 'silence' and 'thought'. The reduction is an explanation of 'expression' as 'synchronic' and 'diachronic' language. And, the 'interpretation' is an explanation of 'speech' and 'speaking', i.e. the nature and function of 'communication' as fundamentally 'human'.

The research which led to the present book began while I was pursuing postdoctoral research in the Department of Philosophy at the University of Dundee, and, the Department of Logic and Metaphysics at St. Andrews University, both in Scotland. In addition, I am grateful to my colleagues in the Departments of Linguistics, Philosophy, and Speech at Southern Illinois University whose dialogue with me influenced much of my thinking as the research progressed. I am grateful to everyone involved, but especially to Mr. J. R. Cameron and Dr. Thomas J. Pace. The position I take with my analysis is, of course, my own.

RICHARD L. LANIGAN
26 January 1976

INTRODUCTION

During his inaugural lecture on "Meaning and Truth" at Oxford University in November of 1969, P. F. Strawson took up what was at the time a key problem in the philosophy of language. Professor Strawson formulated the problem as "the conflict between the theorists of communication-intention and the theorists of formal semantics." The significance of Strawson's statement lies not so much in the acknowledgment of competing theories, as in the recognition of the philosophic importance of the interpersonal nature of the communication, that is, the speech act.

In the study that follows, I want to argue that one approach to a philosophical theory of *speech acts* is a phenomenological account of 'meaning' in an existential sense of interpersonal communication that necessarily should go beyond only a logical analysis of what it is for persons to use language as paradigms of sense and reference. Put more exactly, the account to be offered suggests that meaning can be best understood phenomenologically as the mutual 'intentionality', (i.e. Husserl's sense of an object of consciousness) of a speaker and listener, rather than just the logical regularity of two sets of linguistic experience as embodied in sentence forms.

Historically speaking, the theory of speech acts emerged from the writing of John Langshaw Austin, most notably in his posthumous book *How to Do Things with Words*. It is important for the moment to note that Austin hypostatized three types of speech acts. First, there is the *locutionary act* which has *meaning*, and, there is the *illocutionary act* which has a certain *force* in saying something. Third, the *perlocutionary act* achieves a certain *effect* by being said. In this categorization, Austin brings to light several interesting distinctions for 'meaning' within the context of human communication. He separates *constative* statements, which are susceptible to being either true or false, from *performative* statements which in their very utterance are the *doing* of actions *per se*.

Also, he provides a working distinction between those theorists who rely upon philosophic analysis (or the concepts of speech) and those theorists who utilize formal semantics (linguistics or the rules of usage) to explain the nature of 'meaning' within human behavior as manifest in speech. More importantly, Austin raises the question of and suggests the manner in which philosophic analysis should go beyond the purely logical analysis of speech acts to the phenomenological explanation for describing speech as the creation of a total act in a total situation.

Austin's fundamental tenets of the speech act theory have subsequently been analyzed, principally by H. P. Grice's theory of 'non-natural' meaning and the subsequent inclusion of this theory of meaning in J. R. Searle's study illocutionary acts as paradigmatic speech acts of communication. It is precisely Austin's theory and these elaborations that I want to discuss in this study since their limitations suggest the basis for what I am, in the end, suggesting. That is, the thesis that the speech act theory is a necessary first step toward a phenomenology of human communication in that the theory indicates the ways in which a logical account of language as an abstract system (langage) cannot adequately account for the phenomenology of speech (parole) as the communicative behavior of human experience (langue). This is to argue that the distinctions between locutionary, illocutionary and perlocutionary acts while distinct in some logical senses collapse in the end. Rather, the distinctions to be made are on another level of analysis. A phenomenological investigation that begins in description as a static analysis should proceed onto explanation as the dynamic analysis which accounts for the description. In a historical sense, once again, this is to argue that the analytic description is finally dependent upon the dialectic explanation.

In the chapters that follow, we will examine various descriptions of speech acts as communication structures and contents — two analytic dimensions of a state of affairs called the 'speech act'. Such a review necessarily questions the view that speech, even as 'performance', is an object of analysis in a logical, empirical sense. Rather, speech is specified (in the last chapter) as one facet of the regularities of human communicative behavior that accounts for the consciousness of 'communication'. Speech acts on this account are only a part of the object of consciousness which is human behavior generally, or as Searle would say, only a 'form of behavior'. One is left, then, with the thesis that phenomenological analysis is an explanation that goes beyond description (see the Appendix). In consequence, the account that emerges as the object of philosophic analysis is speech as humanly existential within the phenomenon of communication, rather than speech as a linguistic paradigm of only logical significance. This study, then, is a project in philosophic analysis and explication; it is a hermeneutic of those items of knowledge (what is described) which constitute human consciousness in communication by speech acts (what is explained). Thus, what follows is a speech act phenomenology.

CHAPTER I

PHILOSOPHY OF HUMAN COMMUNICATION

Communication is one of the principal criteria for describing activity that is human. The nature and function of language as Man's chief vehicle of communication occupies a focal position in the human sciences, particularly in philosophy. Human communication is problematic from the beginning, because the term is at once a nominative description for varying states of affair, and yet, the term suggests an explanation for the process nature of speech as an activity. Now the shape of a problem emerges. We are faced with an antinomy. Is the apparent happy relationship between the nature and function of language actually contradictory? Or to reformulate the question, is 'communication' a name for both the nature (description) and function (explanation) of language use in human behavior exchange? This is the basic question that the present study seeks to answer. Thus, the focus of the investigation proceeds to focus explicitly on the speech act theory of language use which in fact presupposes a theory of communication, in the same sense that a conceptual structure presupposes a conceptual infrastructure.[1]

The problematic question, then, is the nature and scope of causality in the use of language to communicate between people. The speech act theory as one finds it in the work of Austin, Searle, Grice, and others, is largely an account of language use as a state of affairs (i.e. statements) prescribed and proscribed in rule defined behavior. In the alternate context of communication theory, one finds an account of language use as a process (i.e. speaking) from which a state of affair (a sentence) is abstracted. In short, the speech act theory proceeds within a causality that suggests that meaning or communicative intent is the cause of language use, whereas the communication theory approach utilizes a

[1] The ideas discussed in this chapter appear in abridged form as "The Speech Act Theory of Interpersonal Communication : Stimulus for Research," *Journal of Applied Communication Research*, 3, no. 2 (November, 1975) : 98-101.

view of causation where language use is the cause of meaning or intention. Let us take up these issues in further detail.

Wittgenstein begins *The Blue Book* by asking the question : What is the meaning of a word?[2] He might as easily have asked, as other philosophers have subsequently done, what is the meaning of a sentence? A proposition? A speech act? A linguistic unit? Or even Alston's recent query, "What are we saying about a linguistic expression when we specify its meaning?"[3] In each instance the question is an analytic probe of language for *what* it is as a semantic token. I take this general approach to the philosophy of language as having its contemporary reformulation in the explicit question which opens John Searle's book *Speech Acts*. Searle asks, "How do words relate to the world?"[4] It is just this restatement of the question that allows a shift in perspective. Rather than a concern with the empirical characteristics of the natural occurrence of a language which properly belongs to the study of linguistics, the philosopher takes up the view of utility and its underlying semantic presuppositions. As Rhinelander suggests, it is a case in which "the disposition is to fit thought to words rather than to fit words to thought."[5] This is the sense in which Strawson refers to communicative speech acts which by his definition are expressive of a "communication-intention."[6]

As might be expected, the location of the speech act within the wider frame of reference, i.e. as part of a communication phenomenon, derives from the early work of Austin where he takes account of the use of speech acts. As he explains, a speech act is dependent upon the listener securing *uptake*.[7] This is to say, the audience to which a speech act is directed depends upon an understanding of the meaning and force of an utterance in order for the speech act to be manifest as such. This utility aspect of the speech act theory turns on the manner in which the speech act is expressed, as well as on the way in which it is perceived. Both the phases of expression and perception account for the manner in

[2] Ludwig Wittgenstein, *The Blue and Brown Books* (New York : Harper Torchbooks, 1965), p. 1.

[3] William P. Alston, *Philosophy of Language* (Englewood Cliffs, New Jersey : Prentice-Hall, 1964), p. 10.

[4] John R. Searle, *Speech Acts : An Essay in the Philosophy of Language* (Cambridge : At the University Press, 1969), p. 3.

[5] Philip H. Rhinelander, *Is Man Incomprehensible to Man?* (San Francisco : W. H. Freeman & Co., 1974), p. 32.

[6] P. F. Strawson, *Logico-Linguistic Papers* (London : Methuen & Co., Ltd., 1971), p. 183.

[7] John L. Austin, *How to Do Things with Words*, ed. by J. O. Urmson (New York : Oxford University Press, 1968), p. 115-116.

which a speech act is communicative of sense and reference for the persons involved in the linguistic exchange. Our analysis thus far is summarized by Waismann this way.

How misleading is the very form of the question, '*What* is communicable?', which makes us expect an answer of the form : this and this is communicable (e.g. the structure of the experience), in contra-distinction to that (e.g. its content). It would be better to replace this question by another, namely, 'What makes communication possible?', i.e. 'What are the determining conditions of communication'?[8]

What then are some of the conditions that should be examined? The general concept of speech acts within a communication process rests to a certain degree on the theory of 'non-natural' meaning. This theory was originally put forth by Grice in an article simply entitled "Meaning." In it Grice details a fundamental distinction that occurs in utterances which are intended to communicate information from one person to another. First, there is a natural sense of 'meaning' which appears in sentences of the form "A means (meant) *to do* so-and-so (by x)" where A is a human agent. Natural meaning, thus, has the character of simple nomination where a fact or state of affair is asserted in the utterance of language by a speaker, and, a listener recognizes that this is the case. In contrast to this account of natural meaning, there is a non-natural sense of 'meaning' which is exemplified in sentence patterns of the type "A means (meant) something by x" or "A means (meant) by x that ...."[9] Such expressions of non-natural meaning are different from those that are natural, i.e. the non-natural expressions are *de facto* descriptive in varying degrees. The non-natural expression specifies the speech act as producing a state of affairs, not merely by the utterance of words, but by the uptake feature of the listener's response to the speaker. Non-natural meaning derives from the use of language that *per se* reflects the intention of the speaker in the utterance that he produces. In short, the distinction between Grice's natural and non-natural meaning is akin to the usual difference between language nature and function. As Sprigge suggests,

To know the pragmatic meaning of a sentence-utterance, then, is to know what propositional attitude it expresses, or purports to express. To know the

---

    [8] F. Waismann, *The Principles of Linguistic Philosophy*, ed. by R. Harré (London : Macmillan, 1965), p. 248.
    [9] H. P. Grice, "Meaning" in *Philosophical Logic*, ed. by P. F. Strawson (Oxford : At the University Press, 1967), p. 40.

semantic meaning of a sentence-utterance is to know what objective it is which (or to know some characterization of the objective which) is the object of the propositional attitude which it expresses or purports to express.[10]

Here again we encounter an idea that has its roots in the work of Austin. Grice's theory of non-natural meaning is in many ways a specification of the original distinction that Austin discovered and detailed under the names *constative* and *performative* utterances.[11] The constative expression (speech act) is a statement of description (e.g. a sentence) that is asserted as materially certain, that is, it is a proposition that is open to confirmation or denial as being true or false *per se*.

The performative utterance stands in direct contrast to the constative. The performative is a proposition that is neither true nor false, yet derives its meaning as a proposition from having a certain force as an inherent feature of being uttered. This is to say that the utterance of the statement is itself the basis for interpreting the intention of the speaker. It is the expressed language which allows the listener to achieve uptake, to know what is meant by the articulation of the statement. The performative utterance generates an expectation which the listener recognizes and which the speaker intends should be recognized by the listener.

Following Austin's analysis, both the speaker and listener are attuned to the fact that the utterance cannot be legitimately classified as either true or false. Instead, the performance is either *happy* or *felicitous* where the conditions of performance are met, or, the utterance becomes *unhappy* or *infelicitous* when the performance fails in the expectation for which it was generated. In short, the performative utterance requires certain 'felicity conditions' to count as a successful communication of intention. Yet, one is left with a question that Austin himself recognized and attempted to take account of, namely, that the difference in felicity conditions which mark out the distinction between the performative and constative utterances are inadequate. As he suggests, "We must get a much more general theory of the speech-act before we can set up a well-founded distinction."[12]

[10] Timothy L. S. Sprigge, *Facts, Words and Beliefs* (London : Routledge & Kegan Paul, 1970), p. 133.
[11] John L. Austin, "Performative-Constative" in *Philosophy and Ordinary Language*, ed. by Charles E. Caton (Urbana, Illinois : University of Illinois Press, 1963), pp. 22-54. This is a literal translation of a paper titled "Performatif-Constatif" which Austin delivered at an Anglo-French conference at Royaumont in March, 1958. It should be noted that the Caton edition is the only one that includes the discussion which occurred at the conclusion of Austin's presentation.
[12] Ibid., p. 37.

The original statement of the theory was presented, of course, in the William James Lectures delivered at Harvard University in 1955.[13] During the course of these lectures, Austin goes on the refine the constative-performative distinction by specifying three types of speech acts. These speech acts count as a subdivision of, or an infrastructure for, the performative concept which lies at the center of the difficulties with the notion of 'felicity conditions.'

Performatives are grouped into locutionary, illocutionary, and perlocutionary acts. As Sadock notes, the *locutionary acts* are those which are performed in order to communicate. The *illocutionary acts* are speech acts that are accomplished by communicating one's intent to accomplish them. And, *perlocutionary acts* are acts of communication in which the effects that are intentionally caused by the utterance are the chief function of the act.[14]

Much of the contemporary analysis of Austin's theory has focused on the nature of the illocutionary act. Here, I have in mind the work of Searle, Sadock, and Landesman to name representative authors.[15] Undoubtedly, this focused interest results in large measure from the genetic quality of the illocutionary act as being itself the meaning of an act, rather than being a causality for meaning, which is more the case with locutionary and perlocutionary acts. We should note, however, that Campbell argues rather pointedly that if the context of communication is regarded as problematic for speech acts, then Austin's distinctions between the locutionary, illocutionary, and perlocutionary acts may be seriously questioned.[16] Campbell's main thesis is that the 'effect' of an utterance is not adequately distinguished in the three types of speech acts. Agreeing with this point, Shirley has argued that the lack of clear distinction between the types of acts creates conditions such that a speech act theory of meaning is impossible.[17]

We are now confronted by the central question which this study takes up, namely, whether a general theory of communication is presupposed by the 'speech act theory' as described in major theorists such as

---

[13] Austin, *How to Do Things with Words*, cited above.

[14] Jerrold M. Sadock, *Toward a Linguistic Theory of Speech Acts* (New York : Academic Press, 1974), pp. 8-9.

[15] Charles Landesman, *Discourse and Its Presuppositions* (New Haven and London : Yale University Press, 1972).

[16] Paul N. Campbell, "A Rhetorical View of Locutionary, Illocutionary, and Perlocutionary Acts," *Quarterly Journal of Speech*, 59, no. 3 (October 1973) : pp. 284-296.

[17] Edward S. Shirley, "The Impossibility of a Speech Act Theory of Meaning," *Philosophy and Rhetoric* 8, no. 2 (Spring, 1975) : pp. 114-122.

Austin, Searle, and Grice. In most cases, it has been generally assumed that 'communication' is one of the many possible *effects* of an utterance and consequently of marginal interest. As Strawson illustrates, some theorists take the stance that "as far as the central core is concerned, the function of communication remains secondary, derivative, conceptually inessential."[18] This assertion is in want of testing.

As Campbell's analysis suggests, we should question whether or not the concept of communication is actually the core meaning that is primary, original, and essentially constitutive of the speech act concept. In short, we want to discover if the concept of communication functions with the nature of an infrastructure upon which the speech act concept depends as a structure.

Inasmuch as the speech act theory is also a theory of meaning, it is useful to recall the ways in which meaning may be used in the wider realm of communication that is presupposed by advocates of the speech act account of language use.

We must keep in mind, however, that the sense of what we mean by *meaning* changes significantly in each part of the communication process. *Meaning* as intention (what I intend to do) is not the same sense of *meaning* as *meaning* in the sense of the ideas I intend to communicate. And the meaning of the content of my message is not the same sense of *meaning* as the meaning which convention attributes to my words, for it sometimes happens that my words do not convey my idea. Finally, the interpreted meaning, or *meaning* to the person interpreting my message, can be far from my intended meaning. So while my initial intention to communicate may be said to involve the whole process, including plan of action, a message content, some symbols to express the content, and an interpretation, we must nevertheless recognize that there are still four rather distinguishable senses in which the term *meaning* can be used when discussing the problem of communication.[19]

It should be apparent that when the speech act theory of meaning is examined from a context point of view we are confronted with the fact that the function of Strawson's 'communication-intention' is a composite of four terms (as outlined by Alexander) which creates ambiguity about the concept 'meaning'. Thus, we are at the point of problem confrontation. Exactly how is the speech act theory problematic within the contextual perspective of human communication as a language use process?

[18] Strawson, *Logico-Linguistic Papers*, p. 188.
[19] Hubert G. Alexander, *Meaning in Language* (Glenview, Illinois : Scott, Foresman & Co., 1969), p. 7.

1. COMMUNICATION AS PROBLEMATIC

The philosophic account of human communication that follows in this section of the study is based primarily on the account given by Hubert G. Alexander.[20] His explanation begins with communication as a symbolic and semantic activity that is directly related to the process of thinking. Thinking is taken to specified as abstracting, determining qualities, discovering relations and function, and the acts of imagining and generalizing. Finally, the nature of rational inquiry is discussed in terms of locating the process of defining and the subsequent form of definitions as they relate to the activities of inferring and systematizing thought. This in brief is the tenor of Alexander's complete presentation, but our concern is only with the starting point, i.e. the primary explication of 'communication' as an object of philosophic inquiry.

Before offering a premature definition of communication, that is, an explanation which purports to characterize the human activity of communication as a process, or alternatively as a state of affairs, we need to explore the various elements of communication that must be explained in either case. Or as Austin expresses the point, "The total speech act in the total speech situation is the *only actual* phenomenon which, in the last resort, we are engaged in elucidating."[21]

At the very obvious level of human experience, the word communication suggests four elements. First, there is the communicator, usually performing as a speaker or writer, who sends or causes to be sent a message. Second, the message is received by a second person performing as a listener or reader, sometimes called the communicatee or recipient of the message. Third, one finds the element of exchange or transfer which accounts for the mechanism of transmission and reception of the message. In short and without sophistication, the element of transfer is the human vocal apparatus or, alternatively, the hearing mechanism of the ear. By extension, of course, we include the sense of sight, touch, and so on. Fourth, the message itself is a principal element.

This last element, the message, is perhaps the most complex. It is not so simple as it might appear. It is not unlike communication itself, since

---

[20] Hubert G. Alexander, *The Language and Logic of Philosophy* (Albuquerque : University of New Mexico Press, 1972), pp. 15-32.

[21] Austin, *How to Do Things with Words*, p. 147. Some of the confusions about communication as alternately a process and a state of affairs are discussed in Gilbert H. Harman, "Three Levels of Meaning" in *Semantics*, ed. by D. D. Steinberg and L. A. Jakobovits (Cambridge : At the University Press, 1971), pp. 66-75.

the 'message' can be used to mean a state of affairs or a process or both, if clear distinctions are not operating. This message element is a complex of at least four interconnected factors. First, the message involves an object, event, or situation which is the object of reference. Second, the message involves a conception of this object, event or situation from the viewpoint of both the speaker and listener, or alternatively, the writer and reader. Third, the message involves a set of symbols used to convey the speaker's concept of the object, event, or situation. Fourth, the message involves a way of conceiving for both the communicator and the communicatee that is affected by the background experiences, attitudes, and knowledge of the people involved.

The description offered thus far suggests that communication is basically a state of affairs since the various elements discussed are constituents of a static whole. Essentially, this is a correct assumption as far as it goes. Now, however, we need to account for the process feature of the communication phenomenon which consists of the processes of (1) encoding and (2) decoding. On the abstract level both encoding and decoding are manifest in the same essential relationship between the factors going to make up a message. Alexander utilizes the following schema in which the letter "R" stands for the *referent* or object, event, or situation referred to; the letter "C" represents the *concepts* or manner of conceiving; the letter "S" stands for the *symbol* or set of symbols; and "E" represents the background *experience*, attitudes, and knowledge.

While the relationships described here account for the state of affairs that could be referred to as 'encoding' or 'decoding' in human communication, it would be misleading. Let me explain why.

In the case of encoding, the E factor becomes the background experiences, attitudes, and knowledge of the communicator and in consequence the C factor becomes the communicator's concept (illustrated by "CC"). In addition, the S factor becomes the symbol(s) chosen by the communicator. Last, the referent or R factor becomes the object of perception or imagination of the communicator. These relationships are presented below with the subscript "1" indicating the factors belong to the communicator, hence specify the process of encoding. The arrows suggest the temporal sequence of the process.

$$S_1$$
$$\nearrow$$
$$E_1 \rightarrow CC_1$$
$$\nwarrow$$
$$R_1$$

Thus, while encoding is descriptive of a state of affairs it is also a process chosen or produced by the communicator in a specified manner to mean one of the many possible ways of constructing a message.

Decoding involves the same message factors as encoding, except that the relationship of the factors is reversed as a process. This is to say that the S factor becomes the symbol(s) as understood by the comunicatee. And, the R factor is likewise the referent as perceived or imagined by the communicatee. The C factor is changed to "CC" (as in the case of encoding) since the concept is now that of the communicatee alone. Also, the E factor now represents the background of the communicatee. The specification of this relationship as decoding, as the process relation of the message for the communicatee, is indicated by the use of the subscript "2". Again, the arrows suggest the temporal sequence in the process.

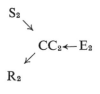

$$S_2$$
$$\searrow$$
$$CC_2 \leftarrow E_2$$
$$\swarrow$$
$$R_2$$

It would be fairly obvious that any theorist will tend to equate the encoding and decoding processes as analogous with the exception that one specifies the view of a speaker and the other the view of a listener. One problematic area would be the link between these two processes in an actual communication situation. The link is the transmission/ reception aspect of the message that was discussed above. In other words, the complete communication process consists of three phases : (1) the encoding, (2) the transmitting and receiving, and (3) the decoding. In this categorization, transmission and reception are taken to imply the link between the speaker and listener and the reverse link in the case

of a listener who responds or reacts. Alexander offers this representation
of the entire communication process :

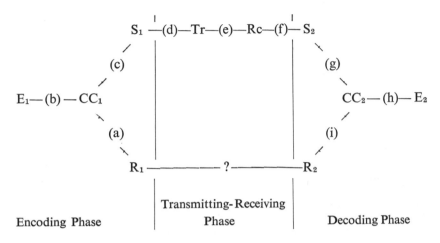

| Encoding Phase | Transmitting-Receiving Phase | Decoding Phase |

Within this model the symbols "Tr" and "Rc" indicate respectively
transmission and reception. The symbol "?" is used to indicate that
response or reaction is possible suggesting concomitant reference. The
symbols "a" through "i" indicate relations that are possible problematic
areas, a point that I will detail in a moment.

At this point it is necessary to indicate, at least in a general sense,
how the speech act theory becomes problematic because of the assumptions it makes about the communication process in which such speech
acts occur. Searle explains of the speech act theory that "this approach
can be characterized by saying that it conceives of the speaking of a
language as a human activity." And that "rather than concentrating on
the linguistic forms, one concentrates on the speech acts that are performed in the utterance of those linguistic forms."[22] Clearly the place
of speech act theory is within the context of communication theory.
Of course, one should recall that the original exploration made by Austin
was very much within the framework of the communication situation.
As he explained very early on in the Harvard Lectures :

Speaking generally, it is always necessary that the circumstances in which
the words are uttered should be in some way, appropriate, and it is very commonly necessary that either the speaker himself or other persons should

_____

[22] John R. Searle, "Human Communication Theory and the Philosophy of Language : Some Remarks" in *Human Communication Theory : Original Essays*, ed. by
Frank E. X. Dance (New York : Holt, Rinehart and Winston, Inc., 1967), p. 119.

also perform certain other actions, whether 'physical' or 'mental' actions or even acts of uttering further words.[23]

One might assume then that the speech act theory takes account of the communication situation, however this is not entirely the case. The speech act theory as presented in the work of Searle presupposes an ideal situation in which the transmission/reception phase of the communication cycle links the encoding and decoding phases as an identity of processes. While this procedure is analytically helpful, it comes dangerously close to assuming what is to be proved.

In order to indicate the nature of this problem area, it is necessary to have a concrete example of the speech act theory before us. Searle's conditions for the successful performance of the illocutionary act of 'promising' is the paradigm that is most useful to our discussion.

Given that a speaker S utters a sentence T in the presence of a hearer H, then, in the literal utterance of T, S sincerely and non-defectively promises the p to H if and only if the following conditions 1-9 obtain :

1. *Normal input and output conditions obtain.*
   I use the terms "input" and "output" to cover the large and indefinite range of conditions under which any kind of serious and literal (fn. I contrast "serious" utterances with play acting, teaching a language, reciting poems, practicing pronunciation, etc., and I contrast "literal" with metaphorical, sarcastic, etc.) linguistic communication is possible. "Output" covers the conditions for intelligible speaking and "input" covers the conditions for understanding. Together they include such things as that the speaker and hearer both know how to speak the language; both are conscious of what they are doing; they have no physical impediments to communication, such as deafness, aphasia, or laryngitis; and they are not acting in a play or telling jokes, etc. It should be noted that this condition excludes *both* impediments to communication such as deafnesss and also parasitic forms of communication such as telling jokes or acting in a play.

2. *S expresses the proposition that p in the utterance of T.*
   This condition isolates the proposition from the rest of the speech act and enables us to concentrate on the peculiarities of promising as a kind of illocutionary act in the rest of the analysis.

3. *In expressing that p, S predicates a future act A of S.*
   (Discussion omitted).

4. *H would prefer S's doing A to his not doing A, and S believes H would prefer his doing A to his not doing A.*
   (Discussion omitted).

5. *It is not obvious to both S and H that S will do A in the normal course of events.*
   (Discussion omitted).

[23] Austin, *How to Do Things with Words*, p. 8.

6. *S intends to do A.*
   (Discussion omitted)

7. *S intends that the utterance of T will place him under an obligation to do A.*
   (Discussion omitted).

8. *S intends (i-1) to produce in H the knowledge (K) that the utterance of T is to count as placing S under an obligation to do A. S intends to produce K by means of the recognition of i-1, and he intends i-1 to be recognized in virtue of (by means of) H's knowledge of the meaning of T.*
   (Discussion omitted).

9. *The semantical rules of the dialect spoken by S and H are such that T is correctly and sincerely uttered if and only if conditions 1-8 obtain.*
   (Fn. As far as condition 1 is concerned, this is a bit misleading. Condition 1 is a general condition on any serious linguistic communication and is not peculiar to this or that dialect. Furthermore the use of the biconditional in this condition excludes ambiguous sentences. We have to assume that T is unambiguous).

   This condition is intended to make clear that the sentence uttered is one which, by the semantical rules of the language, is used to make a promise. Taken together with condition 8, it eliminates counter-examples like the captured soldier example considered earlier. The meaning of a sentence is entirely determined by the meaning of its elements, both lexical and syntactical. And that is just another way of saying that the rules governing its utterance are determined by the rules governing its elements. We shall soon attempt to formulate the rules which govern the element or elements which serve to indicate that the illocutionary force is that of a promise.

   I am construing condition 1 broadly enough so that together with the other conditions it guarantees that H understands the utterance, that is, together with 2-9 it entails that the illocutionary effect K is produced in H by means of H's recognition of S's intention to produce it, which recognition is achieved in virtue of H's knowledge of the meaning of T. This condition could always be stated as a separate condition, and if the reader thinks that I am asking too much of my input and output conditions that they should guarantee that the hearer understands the utterance, then he should treat this as a separate condition.[24]

As can be discerned in the foregoing presentation, there are many complex issues and assumptions at hand. I have retained only those sections of the discussion that Searle presents which bear directly on the issue before us, namely, the presumption of an explicit communication theory as an infrastructure to the speech act theory presented in the paradigm above. The key points of analysis must of necessity revolve around conditions 1 and 9 where the nature of encoding (input) and decoding (output) are integrated within the lexical and syntactic

---

[24] John R. Searle, *Speech Acts*, pp. 57-61.

elements of a sentence. Hence, it is now appropriate to return to Alexander's communication model as a means of systematically discussing the relationships between elements and the comparative relationships being utilized by Searle in each case. By proceeding in this fashion a number of the issues can be articulated which will indicate the problematic nature of the speech act theory within the context of communication theory.

In the discussion that follows reference is made to Alexander's representation of the communication process that occurs above at page thirteen. In all, the relations "a" through "i" are examined. Relation (a) indicates the communicator's concept of the referent, that is, the object, event, or situation to which he is referring. Undoubtedly this relation falls within the scope of Searle's first condition : Normal input and output conditions obtain. Searle would seem to take account of relations (a) and (b) by specifying that his condition one requires that the speaker and hearer know how to speak the language. This condition is obviously circular. A normal, literal *ability to* speak the language is by definition to *know* how to speak. Some qualification, the recognition of relation (c), occurs in Searle's condition nine in which the meaning of a sentence ('sentence' has difficulties in being synonymous with 'utterance') is determined by its lexical and syntactical elements. On a purely theoretical level Searle takes account of relation (a) by stressing a secondary point rather than confronting the primary issue.

A communicator, a speaker in this case, must be able to conceive of the referent. Searle expresses this point as the ability to know how to speak and the ability to distinguish the literal from the metaphorical and the ingenuine from the serious in expression. While these are clear distinctions with respect to the speaker's purpose in specifying relation (b) the coordination of experience and conception (E_1 to CC_1), which is, incidently, the reason for Searle's second condition, there is no explanation by Searle to account for the conceived nature of the referent as literal or serious, or, the reverse case. The key point here is that the specification of an utterance as literal, etc. can only be judged after comparison in a situation where a hearer has responded or reacted in some way. The speaker may intend that his utterance be literal and the hearer may perceive it as metaphorical. A situational judgment is possible only after comparison of speaker and hearer with respect to relations (a) and (i). Namely, does the conceived referent match for both speaker and listener? Searle's conditions do not make clear whether the proposition P is a function of R_1 or R_2, of E_1 or E_2, of S_1 or S_2, or of some combination. In summary, Searle assumes that relations (a) and (i), and (b) and (h), are the same by force of the fact that the same language or dialect can account for a similar description of each (i.e. mean the same thing), since relations (c) and (g) are represented by the same symbol sequence, namely "utterance of T."

At this point, Searle is in the position of suggesting that conceptually the 'encoding' phase with relations (a) (b), and (c) is identical to the 'decoding' phase with relations (g), (h), and (i). We are to assume that since the same structural relationships are present in both phases that the phases are constitutive of a literal and serious utterance. But the assumption is weak for there is no identity of phases, as content, there is merely relational association of the most general kind. As Katz argues :

On this model, the process of linguistic communication is conceived as one in which the speaker, in his production of speech, encodes his inner, private thoughts and ideas in the form of some external, publicly observable, acoustic phenomena, and the hearer, in his comprehension of speech, decodes the *structure* of such objective phenomena in the form of an inner, private experience of the same thoughts and ideas. Language is thus viewed as an instrument of communication of thoughts and ideas which enables those who know the same language to *associate* the same meanings with each of the significant sound sequences in the language.[25]

In other words, Searle's conditions one, two, and nine account for the speaker and listener utilizing a knowledge of the same structure of a language, its syntactical features, but he does not account in an unambiguous way for the semantic features. The semantic features can at best only be analogs, and in a literal sense R_1 cannot count as R_2 nor can the equivocation of "in the utterance of T" function conjointly as relations (a), (b), (c), (g), (h), and (i). Thus in Searle's condition nine, a knowledge of the sentence T, can only count as a structural (i.e. syntactic) recognition for which *any* semantic element is appropriate. We are left with a difference containing no distinction. This is a major reason for being cautious in the equation of 'sentence' as a structural description (i.e. defined syntax) with 'utterance' as structural *and* semantic description (i.e. defined syntax, defined semantics, and consequent definition of the syntactic-semantic relationship).

Sentences are indeed recognizable by native speakers of the language, but such utterances can and do have multiple semantic interpretations. This is the question of "mutual knowledge" as Schiffer refers to it.[26]

[25] Jerrold J. Katz, *The Philosophy of Language* (New York : Harper & Row, Publishers, 1966), p. 176.
[26] Stephen R. Schiffer, *Meaning* (Oxford : At the Clarendon Press, 1972), p. 30 ff.

Searle unsuccessfully attempts to account for this problematic factor (the point of this present analysis) in the footnote to condition nine by saying that "we have to assume that T is unambiguous." As Katz argues, "ideas, thoughts, cognitions, etc., like utterances, are performance phenomena, while meanings, like phonological features and syntactic categories, are abstractions that form part of competence."[27] In saying this Katz affirms that the way in which Searle's condition one counts as 'meaning' (viz. that "normal input and output conditions obtain") can only be taken as a syntactic requirement where relations (d), (e), and (f) account for speaker and listener competence in their dialect, but do not account absolutely for the 'meaning' of an utterance (i.e. coherence of the "encoding" and "decoding" phases).

What is the problematic area for the speech act theory as we have reviewed it above? It comes to a rather simple judgment that carries with it a difficult theoretical implication. Given the nature of the communication process as Alexander's work indicates, Searle's account takes up an explanation of an ideal conception of how a performative speech act works, it does not come to grips with the reality based experience of performance where 'meaning' is more than a structural feature of language. In short, speech is more than language *use*, it is the concomitant expression and perception of language as 'meaning' in each of the four senses specified by Alexander previously where the proposition P can be specified. As Austin notes, "reference depends on knowledge at the time of utterance."[28]

Obviously, Searle puts in several reservations for the investigation of speech acts for ease and clarity in the analysis of performative utterances. In addition, Searle offers little justification for the implicit assumptions upon which he builds his theory. My contention is that in so doing his analysis and explanation of 'speech acts' is so narrow as to be more an exception to the rule rather than the rule in accounting for what a speech act is. A reexamination of the basic methodology appears to be increasingly relevant to the present discussion.

2. PHILOSOPHIC METHOD AND COMMUNICATION

Methodology in a philosophic study such as the present one is a difficult issue because in several relevant senses the method accounts for the

---

[27] Jerrold J. Katz, *The Underlying Reality of Language and Its Philosophical Import* (New York : Harper Torchbooks, 1971), p. 121.

[28] Austin, *How to Do Things with Words*, p. 143.

direction and tenor of the answers being sought. In his work on speech acts, Searle adopted a methodology that derives from the problematic issues just discussed above, i.e. assumptions that syntax in ideal forms can explain 'meaning' in language use. In the study of language one is confronted with questions as to the criteria which must determine the validity of the analysis. Traditionally, the study of linguistics takes as its source of validity paradigm instances of the natural occurrence of the language(s) studied. In a straightforward sense this amounts to saying that the symbols used in a language are direct representations for 'meaning.' Meaning is thereby defined as the linguistic practice, that is, the symbol used in place of either a tangible or conceptual referent.

Taylor has adopted this point of view as a philosophic method, although it legitimately remains an observational methodology properly belonging to the field of linguistics.

To say that something has a meaning, or is a word, is to say it has a use (i.e. someone can teach another to use it) and that the transmission of the skill of using it consists in teaching someone when to use it and when not. Two further conditions are, however, required. First, the possibility of someone using it to produce an effect upon another (except one explicable solely by its physical properties) depends on both having learned how to use it. Second, the conditions under which it is correct to use it cannot in general be described without its use. The use of all words cannot be acquired by verbal instruction or from a dictionary.[29]

With this type of methodology procedure, one can offer descriptions with varying degrees of syntactic, semantic, and phonological accuracy. However, the method does little in a systematic way to provide an underlying explanation for the description offered. To return to a conceptual frame previously mentioned. The methodology being discussed is a descriptive technique that specifies what the language is as a functional activity or tool of communication.

Part of the popularity of this descriptive approach is the ease with which one can argue, as does Chomsky,[30] that self reports of language behavior can with accuracy be generalized to all users of that language. The main point here is that speaking a language is a rule directed activity and that a native speaker knows the rules just as every other native speaker. The obvious shortcomings to such a point of view are the individual differences found in different speakers and hearers of the same

[29] Daniel M. Taylor, *Explanation and Meaning : An Introduction to Philosophy* (Cambridge : At the University Press, 1970), pp. 189-190.
[30] Noam Chomsky, *Aspects of the Theory of Syntax* (Cambridge, Mass. : The M.I.T. Press, 1965), p. 24.

'ideal' language. And, the similarity or uniqueness of natural languages is an open question at the point where the linguist attempts to account for all language behavior with the model of one natural language. But, this latter point is an issue beyond the scope of the present study.

I have suggested up to this point that the description of speech acts as a matter of linguistic practice is tied directly to the process of being taught a language and then assuming that what one has been taught (by description) is the social norm for speaking accurately and effectively. The other side of the question, learning a language by means other than direct instruction, is the quest for an explanation of language *use*. Here I am following the important distinction that Ryle makes between use and usage.[31] It is an important distinction because it is generated out of the context of a communication event. That is, Ryle lays stress on the listener in the situation and takes up not the teaching of a language, but its learning. While this is a subtle distinction, it is nonetheless quite revealing.

A language is something to be known, and we get to know it by learning it. We learn it partly by being taught it, and partly by picking it up. For any given part of a language, a learner may not yet have learned that part; or he may have learned it and not forgotten, or he may have learned it and forgotten it. A language is a corpus of teachable things. It is not, of course, a static corpus until it is a dead language. Nor would two teachers of it always agree whether something should be taught as part of that language.[32]

To view language use as a thing to be learned recognizes that the speaker and the listener are bound into a communication system in which the behavioral rules explain meaning but do not pretend to constitute a complete description that is verifiable as such. Of course, this is precisely the direction in which Austin was moving with his constative-performative distinction. As Findlay expresses it :

Ordinary speech further provides us with an instrument for communicating with others about matters public and common, which is also an instrument for purely personal use, in which different observations, different views, different judgments provide much the same complementary parallax, and the same corrective or confirmatory testing as in the interpersonal case.[33]

[31] Gilbert Ryle, "Use, usage, and Meaning" in *The Theory of Meaning* ed. by G. H. R. Parkinson (London : Oxford University Press, 1968). Cf. Antony Flew, "Philosophy and Language" in *Essays in Conceptual Analysis* (New York : St. Martin's Press, 1966), p. 7 ff.

[32] Ibid., p. 109.

[33] J. N. Findlay, "Use, Usage, and Meaning" in *The Theory of Meaning*, ed. by G. H. R. Parkinson (London : Oxford University Press, 1968), p. 125.

In this discussion both Ryle and Findlay are suggesting that language use is a notion synonymous with 'speech' because as Ryle indicates, "A person who says something senseless or illogical betrays not ignorance but silliness, muddle-headedness, or in some of the interesting cases, over-cleverness. We find fault not with his schooling in years gone by but with his thinking here and now."[34] Now, if we can assume that a clear distinction exists between language usage with its concept of description and language use with its concept of explanation, we can come to an explicit methodology statement for the present study.

Searle points out that in the study of speech acts a distinction needs to be made between (1) talking, (2) characterizing talk, and (3) explaining talk.[35] These three categories represent respectively, the occurrence of speech ("This is a house."), the description of the speech occurrence ("'This is a house' is a sentence."), and the explanation of speech (The use of a noun in the predicate following a pronominal subject requires either a definite or indefinite article following the verb to be). Searle goes on to examine speech acts within the second category alone, assuming in any case that category one is merely the existence of the data to be analyzed. The third category is put aside as a natural consequence of what can be derived from category two as long as the "vaguely defined features as simplicity, generality, and testability" are accounted for in the research statement.

The weakness of Searle's methodology is in beginning from the assumption that "characterizations" are an obvious, discoverable link between referents and symbols that are in the consciousness of the native speaker. As he says, "this method, as I have been emphasizing, places a heavy reliance on the intuitions of the native speaker."[36] In contrast to this point of view, I am suggesting that Searle is correct in the limited sense that the underlying explanation for speech activity is present to the native speaker as part of his inventory of knowledge, but also that this underlying explanation or infrastructure is not static. This is to say, the native speaker has a knowledge, variable in nature as Ryle suggests, which can be described as the linguist does, yet one can and should go beyond this description to explanation which accounts not only for the consistencies of usage, but also its inconsistencies. In short, it should be possible to discover a consistent infrastructure in spite of the occurrence of different acts. In Austin's sense we must dis-

---

[34] Ryle, "Use, Usage, and Meaning." p. 115.
[35] Searle, *Speech Acts*, pp. 14-15.
[36] Ibid., p. 15.

cover "the utterance-*origin* which is used generally in any system of verbal reference coordinates."[37]

In the discussion of speech acts a descriptive analysis tells us *what* an utterance is as an act, which is descriptive of four possible acts : statement, question, command, and exclamation. In addition, there is an explanatory analysis which indicates *how* an utterance is a sentence and in some cases how an utterance is a sentence that is contradictory to the description assumed to be static in the first instance. For example, we may hear the utterance, "This is an automobile." Taken as a description, it is a declarative sentence or statement being utilized to offer information to a listener. Taken as an explanation, it is a sentence being used to communicate in a way that is dependent on the situation, speaker and listener for more information before analysis can proceed. It may be a declarative sentence, yet voice contour in the utterance, for example, may make it into a question or interrogative sentence, and so on. It may be an offer or a request for information, but in any case we are certain that a communication has taken place, that is, a language use that links speaker to listener is the specification of a situation.

Cohen in a very systematic review of the problematic nature of speech acts in the context of social communication suggests five factors in the communication process that display the inadequacy of description without explanation. "First, there are many strings of English words that can have vastly different meanings according to the intonation with which they are uttered." Second, it is quite possible that a sentence with a set grammatical point of view can be uttered with a wide range of meanings. Third, certain patterns of sentences are uttered in common practice with one particular kind of meaning and when they are uttered with another meaning they are mistakenly taken as an additional rather than an alternative meaning. Fourth, "people often do not succeed in producing utterances that are as clear and definite in meaning as they are intended to be." And fifth, "there is the difference between attempted namings, vetoes, excommunications, contracts, conclusions, etc., and successful ones."[38]

In short, the methodology of this study will be one of description to which is added explanation. Here I take explanation to be a systematic account of the elements found in speech as performance within a social

[37] Austin, *How to Do Things with Words*, p. 60; Richard M. Zaner, "On the Sense of Method in Phenomenology" in *Phenomenology and Philosophical Understanding*, ed. Edo Pivcevic (New York : Cambridge University Press, 1975), pp. 125-141.

[38] L. Jonathan Cohen, "Do Illocutionary Forces Exist?" in *Symposium on J. L. Austin*, ed. by K. T. Fann (London : Routledge & Kegan Paul, 1969), pp. 430-433.

situation. In contrast, I take description *per se* to be an abstraction from speech as it is performed, namely, language as a symbol system. Basically the methodology of explanation is one of explication where analysis seeks to display the infrastructure (speech) operating to give the structure (language) its meaning, i.e. how an utterance is abstracted into a sentence token. In an explicit sense, an explanation must not just account for the intuition of the native speaker in an abstracted (hypothetical) situation, but also must suggest the meaning that occurs between a native speaker and a native listener as a matter of social circumstance. What I am suggesting is that explanation takes account of what in the human sciences is traditionally called (1) cognitive meaning, (2) affective meaning, and (3) conative meaning as the key relationships between 'speech' and 'language'.

Description as we have been dealing with it above is an account of cognitive meaning, the idealized 'what' to be understood in analysis as true or false. Affective meaning is basically the province of the psychologist, although the moral philosopher's concern with the distinction of right from wrong or good from evil bears directly on the method of explanation. However, the key aspect of explanation rests directly with conative meaning wherein an expectation (communication-intention) is integral to the speech act and relates to the cognitive and/or affective base of understanding by completing the social situation.

Thus, explanation as a focus of the *how* element of speech acts is a method that goes beyond the static method used by Searle and others to account for the *what* element of speech acts. In another sense, explanation is a method which depends upon a more exacting description of the language use being investigated. As a justification for the methodology of explanation, we need to examine the nature of 'speech act propositions' which are a synergistic product of the cognitive, affective, and conative elements of meaning as carried in the speech act. As Landesman suggests :

What is wanted is an explanation of the objectivity or interpersonal nature of discourse. The same statement can be made, the same question asked, the same order given by different speakers at various places and times. The linguistic actions of different persons can issue in identical performative objects. Can this be understood without hypostatizing performative objects, without making them into things that exist apart?[39]

___

[39] Landesman, *Discourse and its Presuppositions*, p. 158.

3. SPEECH ACT PROPOSITIONS

The use of the term 'proposition' is a modern technique of sorts to avoid the misunderstandings, purported or real, which attend the term 'meaning'. While in the section above we discussed in brief three types of meaning, namely, cognitive, affective, and conative, we also developed our analysis along the lines that they had some basic characteristics in common, that in fact some genetic element called 'meaning' was indigennous to all. Searle as a typical theorist avoids any direct statement of what meaning is, which of course would be to offer an explanation. Rather, he limits himself to simple description. "Whenever two illocutionary acts contain the same reference and predication, provided that the meaning of the referring expression is the same, I shall say the same proposition is expressed. (Fn. This states a sufficient but could not state a necessary condition. Existential statements, e.g., have no reference.)"[40] And further along in the discussion he adds : "Stating and asserting are acts, but propositions are not acts. A proposition is what is asserted in the act of asserting, what is stated in the act of stating."[41] And finally, "The expression of a proposition is a propositional act, not an illocutionary act."[42]

Although Searle's discussion has the analytic form of a circular definition where a proposition is an expression occurring in a speech act, but is not a speech act, it is an accurate acknowledgement of the elements previously discussed as belonging to the encoding phase of the communication process. A proposition is the relationship that exists between a referent, the conception of that referent, the symbol chosen to represent that referent, and the logic of coherence which unites these elements in time and location. Precisely this definition of a proposition holds for both the speaker and the listener in a communication situation as Skinner has so forcefully argued :

The point that the success of any act of communication necessarily depends on at least a mutual intuiting by S (speaker) and A (auditor) of a whole complex of conventions, social as well as linguistic, about what can and cannot be stated, what sorts of meanings and allusions can be expected to be understood without having to be explicitly stated at all, and in general what criteria for the application of any given concept (for example, that of warning) are conventionally accepted as applying in that given situation and society. I have

---

[40] Searle, *Speech Acts*, p. 29.
[41] Ibid.
[42] Ibid.

sought to argue that this is no less true, but only less evident, in the standard synchronic situation.[43]

While Skinner's comments allude to the nature of the proposition as a factor in the communication act, it is Ayer who has demonstrated rather concisely that the proposition is an inherent part of the speech act since the proposition will always be present in communication as the object of belief. In this case, the object of belief, the proposition, is the coincident relationships expressed by the speaker and perceived by the listener as the encoding and decoding processes of the communication act. As Ayer illustrates this point :

I suggest, then, that the meaning of indicative sentences can be analyzed as follows : given that S is a sentence, p a proposition, and A a person, S means p to A if and only if A's assenting to S is constitutive of his believing that p. It is not of course implied that A does actually believe that p; all that is required is that if he did believe it his assent to S would be constitutive of the belief.[44]

At this point we need to return to Searle's account of propositions and reanalyze its key features. Searle was limited to some degree in the claim that he could make for his description of propositions because of the nature of existential statements as having no reference. Given the distinctions that have previously been made between description and explanation as a methodology which generally follow Strawson's analysis of (1) a sentence; an expression, (2) a use of a sentence; a use of an expression, and (3) an utterance of a sentence; an utterance of an expression, it seems an unnecessary move to deny that existential statements have reference, especially in Strawson's sense of a "uniquely referring use."[45] This point is even more plausible in the wider context of a communication act where the existential statement by the speaker is perceived by the listener as an existential statement, but also perceived as one which 'refers' to the speaker, i.e. points out the speaker as the source of the utterance.

So the point to be made is this : a proposition by Searle's definition, i.e. definition by description, can be a necessary and sufficient condition

[43] Quentin Skinner, "Conventions and the Understanding of Speech Acts," *The Philosophical Quarterly*, 20, no. 79 (April, 1970) : 137.

[44] A. J. Ayer, *Metaphysics and Common Sense* (London : Macmillan and Co., Ltd., 1969), p. 45.

[45] P. R. Strawson, "On Referring" in *Essays in Conceptual Analysis* ed. by Antony Flew (New York : St. Martin's Press, 1966), p. 21 ff. Searle's objection to existential statements is not well founded in a phenomenological sense which is suggested in Chapter V of this study.

of meaning within the context of the utterance of a sentence in a *communication act*. Thus, we have a legitimate argument, or if you will, a justification for the existence of a propositional act. For if the expression of a proposition is a propositional act, not an illocutionary act, then the propositional act is by definition the communication act. The propositional act is not an illocutionary act since that act is bound (for its existence) to the speaker as an action, yet it carries meaning for the listener and is more than a description. The concept of the propositional act serves to explain the speech act as it occurs in a given situation. It is in this sense that Ayer's indicative sentence becomes an utterance with meaning, which accords with Strawson's move from the utterance of a sentence to the utterance of an expression. And here we meet in an uncomplicated way Searle's "principle of expressibility," viz., whatever can be meant can be said.[46] The principle itself is a etiolated recognition (1) that expression as an encoding process of communication is concomitant with and dependent upon the perception process as decoding, and (2) that the communication act is a more exact account of the speech act. In methodological terms, we have discovered that what can be described can also be explained. As Hospers suggests, our analysis puts us in the position of declaring simply that "we have explained by description, if you will; but certainly we have explained."[47]

In point of fact, the general argument concerning explanation that Hospers advances requires two features. First, deducibility which is a necessary condition but not always a sufficient one; and second, there is the requirement for differential application (my term since Hospers offers no labeling name), i.e. the power to explain a wide range of phenomena other than those it was evoked to explain. To bring these criteria into the discussion of speech act propositions is a matter of recalling the nature of propositions according to Searle.

Propositions, according to the account offered by Searle, are first of all "deducible," i.e., when two illocutionary acts contain the same reference and predication the same proposition is expressed in each. In addition, propositions are differentially applicable which is to say, a proposition is what is asserted in the act of asserting and what is stated in the act of stating. Therefore, the expression of a proposition is a 'propositional act,' not an illocutionary act by Searle's analysis.

Finally, we need to recall that the basis for Searle's analysis of speech

[46] Searle, *Speech Acts*, p. 19.

[47] John Hospers, "What is Explanation?" in *Essays in Conceptual Analysis* ed. by Antony Flew (New York : St. Martin's Press, 1966), p. 118.

acts is a 'hypothesis' in Hosper's sense, a hypothesis which states that "speaking a language is engaging in a rule-governed form of behavior."[48] As Hospers comments :

We have said that we explain particular events in terms of laws, and laws in terms of wider laws. But sometimes we give at least tentative explanations of them in terms not of laws but of general *hypotheses* : if a law is a well-established statement of how nature works, a statement about nature's workings that is not well-established, or perhaps not even probable but only possible, cannot be a law.[49]

By this standard Searle's account of propositional acts should be treated as a statement about the speech acts as a rule-governed form of behavior. And in consequence, we should be alerted to the fact that such behavior is specified as a 'form' which immediately signals that at least one alternative form, if not more, is possible. The point at issue here is the possibility that Searle's hypothesis may be confirmed in a wider or different sense by indicating that rule-governed behavior may account for propositional acts as communication acts that confirm or reject the acts as rule-governed behavior.

The present issue can be clarified by looking at Searle's discussion of his hypothesis and then suggesting the manner in which the communication act perspective accounts for propositional acts which are not necessarily examples of rule-governed behavior. Searle reminds us :

I have said that the hypothesis of this book is that speaking a language is performing acts according to rules. The form this hypothesis will take is that the semantic structure of a language may be regarded as a conventional realization of a series of sets of underlying constitutive rules, and that speech acts are acts characteristically performed by uttering expressions in accordance with these sets of constitutive rules.[50]

He proceeds to indicate that the statement of such rules for the performance of a speech act allows one to test the hypothesis and thus arrive at a proof for the validity of the hypothesis. If we could agree (which is improbable) that the 'semantic structure of a language' is an acceptable description of 'communication,' then it becomes clear that there could be a possibility that communication is present within a non-conventional realization of a set of rules or within an act that is *uncharacteristic* of usual or normal performance. In short, the presence of a propositional act within a speech act does not depend upon the speech act as a perfor-

---

[48] Searle, *Speech Acts*, p. 22.
[49] Hospers, "What is Explanation?," p. 100.
[50] Searle, *Speech Acts*, pp. 36-37.

mance making use of a constitutive rule; the exception to the rule may equally well carry the propositional act. As Cameron suggests :

There are certain relationships between words and things, in the world such that a particular sequence of words, in a particular context, will "stand for" or signify a particular possible situation or event : this is how a sentence-token comes to signify a configuration. The signifying relation here is time-indepen-dent because it rests on permanent relationships between word- or sentence-types, possible contexts of utterance, and the world : it is a relation between *possible* sentence-tokens and configurations. And a speaker, in uttering a sentence-token, makes use of this (antecedently existing) relationship between token and configuration, employing the sentence-token as an instrument with which to single out the configuration he is concerned with.[51]

Thus, propositions are a feature of communication acts representing a wider and varying form of rule-governed behavior which necessarily includes the exception to or intentional violation of those institutional rules. The study of the syntax of any natural language is illustration enough of this point, i.e. an explanation for an inconsistent application of a 'rule' is a description of the rule that is violated in the given case.

I have undertaken to examine the scope of the philosophy of human communication in this chapter and in so doing several issues emerged which are dealt with progressively in the chapters that follow. In the discussion thus far, we characterized communication as problematic in the sense that the relationship between speaker, listener, and message is neither a state of affairs nor a process as it contains aspects of both. While the tendency among theorists is to pursue the analysis of speech acts in their static version, communication theorists have tended in the opposite direction. It is clear, however, that in the philosophic distinction between description and explanation there is a vehicle for uniting the two tendencies. By moving from description to explanation, there is the possibility of specifying the nature and function of speech act propositions as the meaning to be found in human communication. In the next chapter, we will examine in some detail the structure of speech acts as a first step in the integration of the speech act theory into a phenomenological communication theory.

---

[51] J. R. Cameron, "The Significance of Speech Acts and the Meaning of Words," *The Philosophical Quarterly*, 20, no. 79 (April, 1970) : 116-117.

CHAPTER II

SPEECH ACT STRUCTURES

The methodological distinction that I wish to draw between description and explanation derives from two basic concepts relative to language. One is that all language and speech display both structure and content. In this chapter, we will analyze the nature of structure as it pertains to language use or speech acts. The question of content we will examine in the next chapter. 'Structure' is a commonly used term and one that has become popular with the emergence of the Continental theories of 'structuralism' which are social and human science applications of a more or less formal linguistic model of behavior. This fact need not concern us beyond the notice that the present discussion is in no way related to any of the structuralist theories.

Speech acts contain what I would like to call 'structure' in that they display various types of semiotic relationships which are themselves definitive, i.e. descriptive, of what they are in fact. Some of these semiotic relationships are overtly contained in the sentences (or words that make up the sentences) as uttered by a speaker, and as such can be labeled a speech act structure. Typical relations that specify such a structure are those studied by Austin in the first instance, namely, 'constatives' and 'performatives.' But there is another degree or level of structure that is not overtly present as a 'brute fact' in such utterances as constatives and performatives. Here, I refer to the rules and conventions of usage that constitute or regulate the appropriate use of utterances in given use situations. These I would like to refer to as the 'infrastructure' of the speech act, because in a very direct sense they are a part of the speech act structure, yet they are not a material part in the sense of being an overt constituent of the verbal or inscribed utterance.

What then will constitute a 'speech act structure?' I would like to argue that the structure and infrastructure as a synergistic unit account for the fact that speech, uttered in a certain way and under certain conditions, is an 'act.' Such a description of speech acts will be an account of *what* constitutes them. As Ware comments :

More needs to be said about what it is to specify or to describe an act. We need to know what the difference is between saying (or specifying) what a person did and describing what a person did — or for that matter explaining what a person did. We should not be misled into thinking that describing what someone did is describing something which someone did.[52]

Having accomplished such an analysis of the speech act as a synergism, we will then be in a position to examine the way in which speech acts function and count as actions or states of affairs growing out of the utterance process. In short, we will be combining the static and dynamic features of speech acts as a means of communication with subsequent epistemological overtones.

1. CONSTATIVES

The word 'constative' is of course a well known invention, along with 'performative,' of Austin, but it is not a trivial contrivance. As he suggested, "It was for too long the assumption of philosophers that the business of a 'statement' can only be to 'describe' some state of affairs, or to 'state some fact,' which it must do either truly or falsely."[53] Or as he was to remark later on, "The constative utterance, under the same name, so dear to philosophers, of *statement*, has the property of being true or false."[54] So, one is left with the query, why the invention of a new name for 'description' or 'statement'? It is, Austin suggests, simply a matter of recognizing that "not all true or false statements are descriptions." In fact, he argues :

Along these lines it has by now been shown piecemeal, or at least made to look likely, that many traditional philosophical perplexities have arisen through a mistake — the mistake of taking as straightforward statements of fact utterances which are *either* (in interesting non-grammatical ways) nonsensical *or else* intended as something quite different.[55]

The type of exception that Austin was thinking of is the 'performative' utterance in which case the utterance *is* the performance of the action

---

[52] Robert Ware, "Acts and Action," *Journal of Philosophy*, LXX, no. 13 (July 19, 1973) : 416.

[53] Austin, *How to Do Things with Words*, p. 1.

[54] Austin, "Performative-Constative," *Philosophy and Ordinary Language*, p. 22.

[55] Austin, *How to Do Things with Words*, p. 3.

(e.g. to utter "I promise" is to perform the action of promising) and hence the question of truth or falsity is not a relevant issue. But we will have more to say about the performative in a moment. The point to be made, however, is that the constative and performative appear to be two types of a class or perhaps two species of the same genus of utterances. The fundamental criterion for distinguishing the types has been the nature of the constative, since it carries with it the available test of confirmation or denial vis-à-vis objective reference to a state of affairs. So that in the end, theorists are left with speculations about the nature of the thing and application of the term of performatives as unknown or ambiguous by comparison with the constative. But, is this optimism about the stability and reliability of the definition of 'constative' justified?

Part of the answer to this question is located in the nature of a statement. A statement is an utterance which asserts the truth of or ascribes a purpose to a state of affairs. Obviously, the truth or falsity of the assertion, ascription, or reference can be determined by comparing the utterance to the original person, event, or activity talked about. Apparently, the role of a constative utterance is to function or be used to accomplish some expression of a state of affairs which will contrast with the function of a performative which is to be or bring about the state of affairs. Austin sets out to find this functional difference associated with a grammatical distinction to be found in sentence forms and their uses. But as Sesonske argues, "It is also time we abandoned forever the notion that functions are exclusive, that e.g., a performative cannot also be a constative, and recognized that many, perhaps most, utterances function in several ways — they have a good deal of interesting business, as Austin occasionally noticed."[56]

And, it is of some consequence that Searle has incorporated, though not always satisfactorily, the notions of reference and predication into his discussion of performatives in their illocutionary and perlocutionary varieties. In other words, much of the work that could be expected of the constative is in fact recognized as appropriate to the performative. Searle does confirm this functional scope of application in his reference to "the constative class of illocutionary acts."[57]

---

[56] Alexander Sesonske, "Performatives," *The Journal of Philosophy*, 62, no. 17 (September 9, 1965) : 460.

[57] Searle, *Speech Acts*, p. 68.

2. PERFORMATIVES

The performative utterance, as just mentioned, *is the doing* of the act. In the famous example, uttering the words "I promise" is the act of promising; it is the making of a promise. Customarily, it is admitted that such utterances are neither true nor false, although they may be sincere or insincere among other things. Thus, the doing of an act simply occurs in using language and there is no question as to whether the words are true or false, since the language simply is that which is uttered. Such an analysis is a focusing once again on the structure of the speech act by referring to its context of utterance. "But suppose we start at a different place, with the *speech situation as such*, and ask, What sorts of things go on here?"[58]

Sesonske maintains, as we did in the first chapter, that "the functions of language may usefully be distinguished in terms of the effects of speech acts on human relations; and particularly that the notion of performatives can be made clear this way."[59] He proceeds to indicate that there are three sorts of relations, or what I am calling structures, involved in the speech act as performative. First, there are *psychological relations* which include both the cognitive and emotive. The two are analytically separable, yet functionally occur together. To borrow Sesonske's example : "If X is acquainted with Y, knows Y is a botanist, loves, hates, or is annoyed with Y, then X is psychologically related to Y."[60]

The second general class of relations or structures is 'generative' which is an action of one utterance brings about some action or state in another. While apparently this is a causal description, Sesonske is careful to point out that the action or state so produced is not a 'result' (i.e. an 'object') but rather a 'response' (i.e. an 'object of consciousness'). His point is the same as that which we introduced with the notion of communication theory, namely that the specification of a state misses the point that a process is involved wherein the relationship of the parts (i.e. utterance *and* meaning) is philosophically more interesting than the uniqueness of this or that part (i.e. utterance *or* meaning).

The third structure is for Sesonske the *'formal'* relation. Two persons are formally related when the range of appropriate or permissible interaction between them is part of the society's or culture's conventions

---

[58] Sesonske, "Performatives," p. 461. (Italics mine.)
[59] Sesonske, "Performatives," p. 462. (Italics mine.)
[60] Ibid.

and rules for behavior. Sesonske's summary analysis of this relation and the previous two is that the performative speech act is a performance of a conventional act. Yet, all speech acts are this and we are left with a conclusion that suggests neither difference nor distinction in the nature or function of speech acts. However, there is an additional performative feature related to function that does mark out the performatives. Specifically, a performative utterance *alters* the formal relations. So we are left with this definition of a performative : "A performative is an utterance whose point is to alter formal relations."[61]

This approach accords with that of communication theory, for the performative utterance of a speaker is such precisely because it is an act following certain conventions for which there is an appropriate response by or consequence for the listener. The action of the speaker is to alter the situation by performing an act in the utterance. This alteration may be many things, but at a minimum is a communication from one person to another that is the meaning of a *situation*. The nature and phenomenological extensions of such a situation are the subject of Chapter V.

What was Austin's judgement on this point, that is, what is the structural distinction between the constative and the performative if Sesonske is correct in his analysis? The basics of an answer to this question form the bulk of Austin's XI Harvard Lecture. There he reminds us that the original distinction with which he started his analysis was that "(1) the performative should be doing something as opposed to just saying something; and (2) the performative is happy or unhappy as opposed to true or false."[62] Austin ends his analysis by trying to express the dimensions which distinguish the performative and the constative utterances. It is he suggests not actually a matter of distinguishing two poles or category extremes. Rather, he says it is more like a historical development. Specifically :

(a) With the constative utterance, we abstract from the illocutionary (let alone the perlocutionary) aspects of the speech act, and we concentrate on the locutionary : moreover, we use an over-simplified notion of correspondences with the fact — over-simplified because essentially it brings in the illocutionary aspects. We aim at the ideal of what would be right to say in all circumstances, for any purpose, to any audience, etc. Perhaps this is sometimes realized.

(b) With the performative utterance, we attend as much as possible to the

---

[61] Ibid., p. 467.
[62] Austin, *How to Do Things with Words*, p. 132.

illocutionary force of the utterance, and abstract from the dimension of correspondence with facts.[63]

In different language, we might suggest that a constative is an utterance
whose meaning is a correspondence with the facts of experienced reality,
but is a correspondence that operates differentially by taking varying
forms. At times the correspondence is between the language used and
the referent as true or false; at other times the correspondence is between
the language used and the believability or credibility of the language
choice available. It is this last factor that is the aspect of the illocutionary
act which shares some features with the performative. Because, the
performative must be a happy and sincere performance; in a word,
it must be believable.[64]

In the context of the present discussion, one may reasonably argue
that the dimension of believability (i.e. 'uptake') which figures in the
constative and performative utterances is another name for communication. 'Uptake' is a method of specifying that the message communicated
is a state of affairs (hence, constative) or that it is a process (hence,
performative). At certain times in special circumstances, we can conceive
(as apparently Austin did) that the constative turns into the performative.
Hence, the appropriateness of his remark that the speech act is like a
historical development. This sounds very much like the description that
the communication theorist would give of the communication event in
which a speaker begins with his account of the facts (constatives) and
soon discovers in the reactions and response of his listener that he
explained for the listener a behavior (performative). Indeed, much of
the impact of Searle's argument for deriving 'ought' from 'is' depends
on this type of historical development, which is more accurately a
linguistic phenomenology.[65]

The conclusion to be drawn from our analysis thus far is that the
useful hypothesis of distinction between the constative and performative
utterance is only that, a hypothesis. But even its status as a hypothesis
loses force when the search for grammatical features, the necessary
and sufficient proof, is found to be ambiguous. More is to be learned
from the situational factors that surround the use of an utterance.
This is to say that the speech act should be located within the speech
situation. Again, we discover that the constative or statement of fact is a

[63] Ibid., pp. 144-145.
[64] This is the thesis advanced by H. P. Grice, "Meaning," *Philosophical Review*,
66, no. 3 (July, 1957) : 377-388.
[65] Searle, *Speech Acts*, p. 175 ff.

situation where one finds acts of the speaker and listener, and, it is a tacit recognition that this situation and these acts share a common relationship, namely, speech. 'Speech' is itself the specified term for the relation or structure of the state of affairs (language) and the process (utterance) which occur in communication.

In short, I am wanting to say that what Austin discovered in the constative-performative distinction is not two types of utterance, but the utterance as a relationship between persons and situations. In this view 'communication' becomes the description for a structure (a relationship) connecting people and situations in which the utterance indicates the nature and scope of the relationship. The utterance as this type of structure is explained by its own infrastructure. In the case of communication, an utterance in a situation, the infrastructure is the rule and convention which accounts for the communication.

Utterances constitute situations because they express as paradigms a rule or convention, yet the utterance expresses the developmental nature of communication. That is, the utterance represents a structure linking people and situations, but the structure has its 'meaning' because it is exemplified by the infrastructure or relation of abstractions about communication, namely, communication as language and speaking. Words are in part abstractions of experience, they name or otherwise indicate situations that people have lived through. Yet, words are verbal (oral and written) representations for the living that people do. In other words, utterance must jointly represent what people experience and how they experience.[66] The what and the how are the situation and the utterance. The human agent, the person, *is* the what and the how at the infrastructure level, i.e. as an 'object of consciousness' which is prior to there being an 'object' for 'consciousness'. His actions as linguistic acts, for example, specify the relationship between himself and the situation. In the case of Austin's constative, the person uses an utterance to specify a situation in relation to himself and he uses performatives to indicate himself in relation to a situation. It is in this sense that Searle argues that "expressions, not universals, are predicated of objects."[67] The object of expression (of an utterance) is a relationship (structure) as language/speech between a situation and a person. This is the traditional

---

[66] This is the point made by the participants (John Searle, Zeno Vendler, and Paul Benacerraf) in the Speech Act Symposium of the 1962 Oberlin Colloquium in Philosophy, published as C. D. Rollins, ed., *Knowledge and Experience* (Pittsburgh : University of Pittsburgh Press, 1966).

[67] Ibid., p. 26.

source of the distinction between instrumental and expressive uses of language.[68]

Many of the issues that I have raised in this discussion of structural or relational aspects of the speech act can be further clarified by looking more closely at the infrastructure that supports them. The infrastructure of speech acts is fundamentally an account of the nature of rules and conventions as they apply to human communication.

3. RULES AND CONVENTIONS

The primary philosophic interest in rules and conventions as they relate to speech act analysis centers around the distinction in turn founded on a difference that is elucidated by John Rawls as a relationship not unlike the structure-infrastructure relation we have been discussing. Rawls argues that there are two ways of looking at rules. First, there is the 'summary view' of rules in which a rule is defined as a summary of past decisions arrived at by the direct application of a utilitarian principle to particular cases. Second, there is the 'practice view' of rules in which rules are seen as defining a practice. In a more particular sense, the rules of practices are logically prior to particular cases and, one can say, are constitutive of the particular case as an action.[69] It is this very paradigm that Searle uses in his attempt to explain the structural nature of speech acts.

Searle, like Rawls, argues that there are two types of rules. 'Regulative rules' and 'constitutive rules' which are distinguishable on logical grounds. "Regulative rules regulate a pre-existing activity, an activity whose existence is logically independent of the rules. Constitutive rules constitute (and also regulate) an activity the existence of which is logically dependent on the rules."[70] In short, Searle is using Rawls' 'summary view' as analogous to his 'regulative rule' while the 'constitutive rule' is comparable to the 'practice view'. Keeping in mind that Austin suggests that a historical movement is involved with this aspect of the speech act, Searle notes that constitutive rules do the same work as regulate rules and that the former necessarily grow out of the latter.

[68] Charles L. Stevenson, *Ethics and Language* (New Haven : Yale University Press, 1960), pp. 62 ff. and 212 ff.

[69] John Rawls, "Two Concepts of Rules" in *Readings in the Theory of Action*, ed. by N. S. Care and C. Landesman (Bloomington and London : Indiana University Press, 1968), pp. 306-340.

[70] Searle, *Speech Acts*, p. 34.

What we have, then, are not two categories of rules, but a difference in degree of application. Or, in the language I prefer to use, we have not two structures, but two infrastructures which account in varying ways for the same structure. It does not lead us to any enlightening discoveries to attempt to describe the logical differences between regulative and constitutive rules as logical types when we are in want of an explanation for what counts as a rule *per se*. "What matters, however, is the distinction between a species of rules with variable application which I shall call 'initiated rules', in which what brings the rule into effect is the action of some person (normally with the intention of bringing a rule into effect) and all other rules."[71] Combining Searle's analysis with that offered by O'Neill, we might argue that an 'initiated rule' is a structural relationship between a person and the action performed in the speech act. As a simple account of the initiated rule, we would call it by Searle's name a regulative rule because "behavior which is in accordance with the rule could be given the same description or specification (the same answer to the question "What did he do?") whether or not the rule existed, provided the description or specification makes no explicit reference to the rule."[72] This is to argue that Searle's regulative rule is the infrastructure of O'Neill's initiated rule taken as a structure.

On the other hand, the initiated rule can equally be called the constitutive rule (or system of rules) because it is "behavior which is in accordance with the rule (that) can receive specifications or descriptions which it could not receive if the rule or rules did not exist."[73] In short, O'Neill's analysis confirms in a different way the original analysis offered by Rawls. This is to say, the generation of rules (especially in the context of a system) is a linear progression from the summary view/regulative to the practice view/constitutive, but not the reverse. Rawls and Searle indicate the state of affairs which account for rule generating behavior, while O'Neill specifies the process of rule generation from the regulative to the constitutive.

An additional justification for the point that rules represent a structure that names a process rather than a state of affairs is offered by Wheatley. He argues that rules belong to one category or structure with a dual infrastructure. Specifically, rules are (1) 'engagement rules' which indicate the necessary conditions for what would be the 'happy' use

[71] B. C. O'Neill, "Conventions and Illocutionary Force," *The Philosophical Quarterly*, 22, no. 88 (July, 1972) : 231.

[72] Searle, *Speech Acts*, p. 35.

[73] Ibid.

(following Austin) of a word, or (2) 'entailment rules' which give the necessary conditions for the 'correct' use of a word.[74] In the same way that Searle argues for his regulative-constitutive distinction, Wheatley maintains that engagement rules presume entailment rules and not conversely. Yet, Wheatley suggests in parallel with O'Neill that a degree scale of use is involved rather than a difference of kind in rules. Let me point out in passing that Ganz also uses the distinction between 'rule' and 'description' to make the same arguments that Wheatley, O'Neill and I want to make.[75]

In terms of speech acts as communicative behavior, we must reformulate Searle's principle of expressibility that whatever can be meant can be said since speaking a language is a *rule-governed* form of behavior. I would, in parallel fashion like to rename the principle as the 'principle of communication'. Specifically, I would prefer to argue that what can be meant can be said because speaking a language is a *convention-governed* form of behavior which we experience as 'communication'. Here, I distinguish 'convention-governed' from Searle's 'rule-governed' which for him means 'rule-constituted'. Searle chooses to emphasize the states of affair that occur in a speech act situation presupposing the conditions necessary for communication.[76] I am attempting to emphasize the process that leads from the 'summary view'/regulative rule to the 'practice view'/constitutive rule. Extending the analysis, 'convention' is the name I use for this description of process which we can further explain as a matter of entailment by designating either a regulative or constitutive rule in Searle's sense. And in the same fashion, we may equate my 'convention' with O'Neill's 'initiated rule'. As Lewis argues, "The *regularity* whereby communicators and audiences use such a pair of contingency plans is a *convention*."[77] Such 'regularity' is not a formal limitation and hence not a 'rule'.

It is important to note that the move back from an inclusive notion of rules, that in a formal sense accounts for all speech act structures, to the simpler infrastructure account allows a better understanding of the speech act. Where we are able to concentrate on the process nature of rule-application in contrast to the static nature of rule-function,

[74] John Wheatley, *Language and Rules*, (The Hague and Paris : Mouton and Co., 1970), p. 35.
  [75] Joan Safran Ganz, *Rules : A Systematic Study* (The Hague and Paris : Mouton and Co., 1971).
  [76] Searle, *Speech Acts*, p. 16.
  [77] David K. Lewis, *Convention* (Cambridge : Harvard University Press, 1969), p. 125. (Emphasis mine.)

we permit a more rigorous explanation of communication as speech acts. As Searle's latest research effort suggests, there is a methodological advantage to be gained by avoiding the analysis of speech acts within a strict format of constitutive rules.[78] In particular, the analysis of the infrastructure of the speech act rather than its structure, i.e., its conventional rather than its rule (constitutive) features, allows one "to distinguish meaning from communication, instead of identifying them as most intentionalist theorists, myself included, have done...."[79] In other words, "What is represented is a state of affairs, but what is communicated is not a state of affairs, but one might say, the representation of a state of affairs."[80]

We have come back to the point at which Austin discovered that the constative-performative distinction was a stage in a historical process. We are saying in the present analysis that the regulative-constitutive distinction exemplifies a historical process that parallels by way of explanation the meaning-communication distinction. That is, meaning and communication are not categories, but from a process in which meaning leads to communication, but communication does not always result in meaning. This is essentially the difficulty that Black first investigated and the one to which Searle has returned as noted above.[81] As Ziff claims :

Rules have virtually nothing to do with speaking or understanding a natural language. Philosophers are apt to have the following picture of language. Speaking a language is a matter of engaging in a certain activity, an activity in accordance with certain rules. If the rules of the language are violated (or infringed, or broken, etc.) the aim of language, viz. communication, cannot save *per accidens* be achieved.

...

Such a picture of language can produce, can be the product of, nothing but confusion.[82]

Along with Searle, we have discovered that the assumption that meaning and communication are more or less synonymous is erroneous. This was to assume incorrectly that the infrastructure of meaning

[78] John R. Searle, "Meaning, Communication and Representation," unpublished paper delivered at the American Philosophical Association-Western Division Meeting at Chicago, Illinois, April 26, 1975. Mimeographed, p. 22.

[79] Ibid., p. 24.

[80] Ibid., p. 6.

[81] Max Black, "Austin on Performatives" in *Symposium on J. L. Austin*, ed. by K. T. Fann (London : Routledge and Kegan Paul, 1969), pp. 401-411.

[82] Paul Ziff, *Semantic Analysis* (Ithaca, New York : Cornell University Press, 1960), pp. 34-35.

constituted the final structure of communication. In point of fact, it appears at least for the present state of analysis that communication is the infrastructure that generates the structure of meaning. Specifically and to draw our analysis together, it is the convention (exemplified in speech act use) that generates the rule (exemplified by speech act usage) — if one must account for the rule at all and this is the point Searle wants to make.[83] While 'convention' is linked to communication and speech 'acts', 'rule' should be linked to meaning and speech 'activities'. Yet, this reverse in the sequence of implication is not the central fact to be investigated.

Rather, as has been our constant argument, the object of investigation is the relationship in the state of affairs. This relationship or structure is not a rule, but a convention, that is, a regularity of communicative behavior. The regularity can account for the way in which a speech act counts as a message between persons, i.e. a communication, without being a description of activity open to disproof by counter-example.[84] As Lewis so forcefully makes the argument : 'For me there cannot be two interpretations of the same language; but there can be two languages with the same sentences.'[85]

Let us review, for the moment, where our analysis has taken us thus far. We began with the problem of distinguishing a constative from a performative. This distinction appeared to depend on separating out utterances (sentences exemplifying generalizations) that were open to counter-example in the first instance (a truth-falsity criterion) and then later with the added element of rules and conventions utterances were open to contextual misuse (a performance criterion). We discovered in this analysis that constatives and performatives actually were both illocutionary acts in the sense that different senses of performance were involved. Here 'performance' describes all the elements of a communication, rather than selective parts that lead to the confusion of constative and performative as speech act types. With the specification of conventions as one end of a process leading to rules as a formal entity, the misconception with speech act structure and infrastructure brings to light the related constative-performative ambiguity. In short, we may say of speech acts at this juncture that they are communications between

[83] Searle, "Meaning, Communication and Representation."
[84] See Christopher Cherry, "Regulative Rules and Constitutive Rules," *The Philosophical Quarterly*, 23, no. 93 (October, 1973 : 301-315.
[85] Lewis, *Conventions*, p. 162. Cf. Skinner, "Conventions and the Understanding of Speech Acts," p. 137.

people that establish situations. These situations are open to description, that is, what the speaker says, what the listener understands, what is true or false, and what is successful or faulty action can be investigated as ways of determining a 'meaning'. Yet, these concepts of meaning leave us with very little knowledge of what a speech act is in a process i.e. as an account of the relationships (conventions) that unite speaker, listener, and message as a synergistic event. We are then left with the next issue. What in the communication situation is to count as the 'speech act'? If communication is indeed a process creating on-going states of affair, what is the nature of an individual act of utterance?

4. LOCUTIONARY ACTS

Before moving to a more or less direct answer to the question that I have posed, let me first suggest that a great deal of importance can be attached to an ordinary-language analysis of Austin's selection of the name 'speech act' as a description-explanation of his linguistic phenomenology. He could have simply used the static name 'language act' or Alston's 'linguistic act' which has the implication of an action *in* words and therefore does not require that any 'effect' occur.[86] Presumably this approach momentarily led Austin to suggest that the illocutionary act was a performance because a certain sense and reference could be accomplished 'in saying' certain words in a given situation. But as Austin subsequently discovered, the sense and reference might equally be contained in a perlocutionary act 'by saying' certain words in certain situations. As a result, the in/by distinction exemplifying an infrastructure in grammar (language) could not adequately account for the structure of communication (speech). In consequence, it is fairly obvious why Austin chose the 'speech act' nomenclature. 'Speech' implies the process in which a state of affairs, an *act*, is generated by a performance. As Austin remarks, "And the more we consider a statement not as a sentence (or proposition) but as an act of speech (out of which the others are logical constructions) the more we are studying the whole thing as an act."[87]

On the other hand, Austin probably spoke of 'speech act' rather

[86] William P. Alston, "Linguistic Acts," *American Philosophical Quarterly* I, no. 2 (April, 1964) : 138.
[87] Austin, *How to Do Things with Words*, p. 20.

than just 'speech' because the latter term implies process.[88] The sense of 'speech act' as the distinctive, yet conjunctive process (action) and state of affairs (act) is not unlike the performative and constative analysis which attempts to refine the distinction of utterance use and usage (speech and language) on syntactical grounds. Austin's attempts to undo this antinomy, not by confronting *how a speech act is a description* (the constative-performative analysis failed on this count), but by explaining *what speech is as an action*. As he is forced to concede :

> Certainly the ways in which we talk about 'action' are liable here, as elsewhere, to be confusing. For example, we may contrast men of words with men of action, we may say they *did* nothing, only talked or *said* things : yet again, we may contrast *only* thinking something with *actually* saying it (out loud), in which context saying *is* doing something.[89]

At this point, Austin moves to construct an answer to our previous questions, viz. What in the communication situation is to count as the 'speech act'? And, if communication is indeed a process creating on-going states of affair, what is the nature of an individual utterance? In his analysis, Austin answers the last question first by attempting to specify the classes of individual utterances or locutionary acts as a means of determining what the genus 'speech act' is.

4.1. *Phones*

Austin asserts that "to say anything is always to perform the act of uttering certain noises (a 'phonetic' act), and the utterance is a phone."[90] We are led in Austin's later discussion of utterance acts to suppose that what he has in mind for the phonetic act is something like the utterance of words, in its simplest sense. This is to say, noises uttered in a conventional way as a 'summary view' (i.e. 'regulative') of rule behavior. This is in fact a way of indicating that utterances have a reference value, irrespective of the questions associated with the 'sense' of the utterance. This is the same structural feature that Alexander describes as the relationship between a communicator's concept and the symbol used, as we discussed in the previous chapter. Or likewise, this is the primitive notion of 'representation' that Searle attempts to distinguish from 'meaning' and 'communication'.[91]

---

[88] Sir Alan Gardiner, *The Theory of Speech ond Language* (Oxford : At the Clarendon Press, 1951), pp. 64-65.
[89] Austin, *How to Do Things with Words*, p. 92.
[90] Ibid.
[91] Searle, "Meaning, Communication and Representation," p. 1.

In another view, the phonetic act is (I would argue) what Austin had in mind with his first grammatical distinction as a basis for speech act analysis, namely, the in/by distinction. This is to say that 'in saying' something the speaker is making use of his vocabulary and he is using it to refer, hence he is *doing* something. In Alexander's sense the communicator is now selecting a symbol for a referent as conceived. The speaker is performing; an action is occurring. But, that is all that we can say about it. To say more is to move to the second type of act, the phatic act.

4.2. *Phemes*

When one's investigation moves to the next highest level of speech act analysis, we discover with Austin that :

To say anything is always to perform the act of uttering certain vocables or words, i.e. noises of certain types belonging to *and as* belonging to a certain vocabulary, in a certain construction, i.e. conforming to and as conforming to a certain grammar, with a certain intonation, &c. This act we may call a 'phatic' act, and the utterance which it is the act of uttering a 'pheme' (as distinct from the phememe of linguistic theory).[92].

As Austin suggests further, we recognize immediately that several distinctions appear as between the phonetic act and the phatic act. First, it is obvious that the performance of a phatic act is also the performance of the phonetic act, yet the reverse is not true or we would be confronted with a difference lacking distinction. Second, the pheme is a combination of grammar and vocabulary. And third, the pheme is "essentially mimicable, reproducible (including intonation, winks, gestures, & c.)."[93]

In what ways is the phatic act a more sophisticated utterance than the phonetic act? We said that the phonetic act was essentially an utterance of vocabulary. When such vocabulary is structured, i.e. when the vocables are related to one another, it has the additional property of possessing a grammar, or more specifically a syntax. As such, Austin later suggests that the pheme is a 'unit of language'.[94] And, the chief fault of the pheme is that it can be 'nonsense', or 'meaningless'. By negative definition, we may conclude that where the pheme is not faulted, one has an utterance with 'sense'. But why the comment that the pheme can be reproduced? There are two items of note here. First, only something

[92] Austin, *How to Do Things with Words*, p. 92.
[93] Ibid., pp. 95-96.
[94] Ibid., p. 98.

that is understood can be reproduced with 'sense'. Second, we have an explanation for the second term in the in/by distinction that Austin relies upon. This is to suggest that 'in saying' something, the speaker is utilizing his vocabulary (phonetic act) and grammar (phatic act) to refer (phone) with sense (pheme), he is *doing* something with his utterance. It should be pointed out that the phatic act is a conceptual whole whose parts are vocabulary and grammar, performance *in* and *by* saying something, but *not* any structural or relational item between the constituent parts. The significance of this point will become more clear when we examine the rhetic act.

4.3. *Rhemes*

Accordin to Austin, to say something is "generally to perform the act of using that pheme or its constituents with a certain more or less definite 'sense' and a more or less definite 'reference' (which together are equivalent to 'meaning'). This act we may call a 'rhetic' act, and the utterance which is the act of uttering a 'rheme'.[95] The key word in Austin's discussion is 'definite' as he attaches it to 'sense' and 'reference'. He appears to suggest that a structure or relationship is involved with the rheme which is a linguistic synergism. The relationship between sense and reference in a given utterance suggests a 'meaning' which is not present as merely sense, merely reference, or merely the summary combination of sense and reference. Rather, the rheme is the "unit of speech" and no longer just a unit of language.[96] As such, Austin can now move to a more sophisticated distinction with the performance nature of a speech act. He raises the new distinction between "performance of an act *in* saying something as opposed to performance of an act *of* saying something" which becomes the 'doctrine of illocutionary force'.[97]

In short, we have the following type of utterance distinction. A phone is an utterance *in* saying something, a pheme is an utterance *by* saying something, and a rheme is an utterance *of* saying something. Whereas the first two are causal in nature, the rheme is synergistic and includes the phone and pheme. In Alexander's sense of 'communication' we have the communicator's concept which is a synergism of past experience, symbol, and referent, or, we have the communicatee's (listener's) concept

[95] Ibid., pp. 92-93.
[96] Ibid., p. 98.
[97] Ibid., p. 99.

which is an analogous synergism. In other words, the communicator and message has the same 'reference' value in Austin's sense, yet the 'sense' may or may not have the same value for both speaker and listener. Austin confirms this analysis by suggesting that the typical fault of the rheme is "to be vague or void or obscure, & c."[98] 'Vague', 'void', and 'obscure' are words used to describe relationships which are ambiguous, structures in which there is perceived sense and reference but in which neither has a relationship that is definite. Since Austin parenthetically defines sense and reference as "naming and referring,"[99] it is fairly clear that our analysis is close to his thinking.

At this point then, the nature of a speech 'act' would appear to be an utterance involving sense and reference. Yet, the chief feature so far discovered is not the explicit meaning associated with the terms 'sense' and 'reference', but rather the relationship or structure that they conjointly represent. This structure is basically performance, which is to say the action of a human agent whose intention to communicate with the use of language (in, by, of saying) creates a situation (act) at various levels of understanding (phones, phemes, rhemes) by adhering to the regularities of such communication which may be abstracted logically (conventions), but not generalized (rules). The speech act structure, therefore, is 'performance', i.e. the name for an utterance act (a communication state of affairs), *and* an utterance action (a communication process) which are a historical relationship simply called 'human communication'. 'Human' because the act/action relationship is no more than a regularity, a convention for message exchange. Obviously, we are left the query as to the substance or content of human communication, in a word, its 'meaning'. Because, it is obvious that the structural nature of performance is only one aspect of 'meaning'. This problem is the subject of the next chapter.

---

[98] Ibid., p. 98.
[99] Ibid., p. 97.

CHAPTER III

SPEECH ACT CONTENTS

Recall that in the initial discussion of communication and meaning, Alexander points out that the communicative process has four distinguishable phases or senses of 'meaning'. These are intentional meaning, content meaning (including conceptual, emotive, and active content), significative meaning, and interpreted meaning, resulting from an act of interpretation. These phases of the meaning process form a continuing sequence with mutual, interacting involvement.[100] Or, as Austin suggested in the process of linguistic phenomenology, the movement from being to doing in utterances is a developmental, historical process.[101] In the last chapter, the structure or relation among these types of meaning was explored by looking at the way in which a situation could come to have meaning. This is to say, how a situation can be explained or described as the result of an utterance as an ordinary human behavior. Our analysis was not very fruitful in that 'speech act structure' emerged as only a part of the explanation for the 'meaning' of an utterance.

Traditionally, philosophers on one account have attempted to pursue a line of inquiry to specify by description the *nature* of 'meaning'. The equally traditional and alternative approach has been to examine and to explain the *function* of language/speech. The attempt in both cases is to specify the way in which an utterance can 'count as' understanding, representing, communicating, etc. Part of the reason for moving to this form of analysis, an investigation of function, has been the logical inadequacy of several theories of meaning deriving from various historical sources. While we need not concern ourselves with the history of philosophy on this issue, it is quite necessary to review some of the principal theories of meaning and their descriptive shortcomings. This review

[100] Alexander, *Meaning in Language*, p. 13.
[101] Austin, *How to Do Things with Words*, p. 145.

will serve to indicate in varying degrees the manner in which contemporary theorists have modified or replaced the explanation of standard approaches.

1. MEANING

Linguistics as the science of language makes distinctions on an empirical (natural occurrence) basis between syntactics, phonology, and semantics. This apparently explicit enumeration of the constituents of language in ordinary discourse is no more than saying that language has a structure (its parts fit together), a physical substance (it is a material sound or inscription) and a conceptual content (the coherence of parts as sounds or inscriptions is a mental experience, or substitutes for something like one). No doubt it is somewhat obvious that phonology is something very much like Austin's phonetic act with similar parallels between phatic acts and syntactics, and the same with semantics and rhetic acts. As Ullmann suggests, "in the act of speech, the concrete realization of the language system, sounds are employed to convey meanings, physical phenomena to call up mental phenomena".[102]

In terms of communication theory, the triadic elements are somewhat more clear. Again recalling Alexander's paradigm as discussed in the first chapter of this study, a communication concept is a synergism of a referent, symbol, and background experience. Various theories of meaning have ascribed 'meaning' to each of these elements (speech act content) or to the relationship that exists between them in whole or in part (speech act structure). We should examine each of these attempts at 'meaning' definition as a method for locating the criteria for 'speech act content'.

1.1. Typologies

The best review of historical theories of meaning to appear in recent years is that of Alston in his book on language and his articles for the *Encyclopedia of Philosophy*.[103] Alston suggests that there are three principal types of meaning theory : the referential, the ideational, and

[102] Stephen Ullmann, *The Principles of Semantics* (Oxford : Basil Blackwell, 1957), p. 29.
[103] Reprint edition, 1972, s.v. "Meaning" by William Alston, 5-6 : pp. 233-241; s.v. "Emotive Meaning" by William Alston, 1-2 : pp. 486-493.

the behavioral.[104] In addition, some theorists make a distinction between a referential and use theory of meaning.[105] However, Alston's explanations describe the aspects of referential meaning relevant to our discussion of semantic theory.

The referential theory of meaning identifies the 'meaning' of an utterance with that to which it refers or with the referential connection. Obviously, the referential theory attempts to describe the speech act by suggesting that the reference is either a state of affairs (the object of reference) or a process (the relationship or structure connecting the reference and referent). Alston points out that the former view associated with a state of affairs is the "more naive view" of the two. The basis for this criticism is the questionable theoretical requirement that 'meaning' is the object of reference, which is an adequate account only for referents that are tangible objects. However, in the case of qualities, relationships, common names, etc. the referent cannot be specified in the sense that one can confirm or validate its existence. On this count, then, the "more sophisticated view" that reference is a relationship between the expression and its referent is a better description. This is the view, of course, that Alexander adopts in his theory of communication. And, it carries a certain amount of persuasion.

In Alexander's account, meaning is the structural synergism of the symbol-concept infrastructure relation, the referent-concept infrastructure relation, and the background experience-concept infrastructure relation. We have in this paradigm the explanation that the 'concept' or 'meaning' (or Searle's 'proposition') of the speaker or listener is the relationship among referent, symbol, and past experience. In short, the referential theory of meaning would account for the 'content' of a speech act by pointing to the three interconnected relationships which constitute a process (a generating structure) which, in turn, can be analytically delimited to three states of affair, each arrived at by abstraction from the other two. Schiffer's argument for a condition of 'mutual knowledge' is an attempt to specify this condition (the speech act 'content') on logical grounds alone.[106] The same issue is approached by Lewis as an attempt to explain communication logically as a 'signal' system.[107] Both studies result in an incomplete answer in that they

[104] William P. Alston, *Philosophy of Language* (Englewood Cliffs, New Jersey: Prentice-Hall, 1964), p. 11ff.
[105] Jerrold J. Katz, *The Underlying Reality of Language and Its Philosophical Import*, p. 85 ff.
[106] Schiffer, *Meaning*, p. 30 *passim*.
[107] Lewis, *Convention*, pp. 122-159.

are not able to resolve the apparent contradiction posed by the fact that utterances with meaning have the characteristics of a process and a state of affairs at the same time. In other words, description becomes conditional as to context of utterance (and at times arbitrary with the equivocation of 'structure' and 'content') and in so doing does not account for natural or everyday understandings of 'meaning' through speech acts. The heart of the logical problem is that the same word or symbol may have more than one referent, thereby obscuring the relationship which carries the 'meaning'.

The result of such philosophic inquiry (i.e. Schiffer and Lewis) has been to move to a consideration that is epistemological rather than metaphysical. This is to say, the analytic approach which is most compatible with strictly logical criteria is to argue that referential theory can be stated by saying that two expressions have the same use if and only if they refer to the same object or perhaps refer to the same object in the same way. Here we have introduced the idea of 'use' as an activity which idealizes a speech act situation that is consistent and unvarying. While this precaution illustrates the problem of a word having more than one referent, it does little to explain why different words can have the same referent and yet mean different things. Many of these problems we will examine in the course of later discussion, but for the moment we need to take up the ideational theory of meaning.

As Alston recounts the theory, 'ideational' meaning is traditionally associated with John Locke as an attempt to explain "the instrument for the communication of thought."

For each linguistic expression, or rather for each distinguishable sense of a linguistic expression, there would have to be an idea such that when any expression is used in that sense, it is used as an indication of the presence of that idea. This presumably means that whenever an expression is used in that sense, 1. the idea must be present in the mind of the speaker, and 2. the speaker must be producing the expression in order to get his audience to realize the idea in question is in his mind at that time. Finally, 3. insofar as communication is successful, the expression would have to call up the same idea in the mind of the hearer, with analogous qualifications as to an "unthinking" grasp of what was being said that might hold on some, though not on all, occasions.[108]

As with the referential theory of meaning, we are faced with several logical problems in the account of meaning as ideas. First, as Alston argues, ideas would have to be introspectively discriminable items of consciousness.[109] He suggests that this approach is absurd in the sense

[108] Alston, *Philosophy of Language*, pp. 23-24.
[109] Ibid., p. 25.

that many ideas or mental images are connected with a given word, so that a word does not represent an idea, but many ideas. And there is the converse problem of one idea being represented by many words. We should, however, recall that Austin warns us that "an *actual* language has few, if any, explicit conventions, no sharp limits to the spheres of operation of rules, no rigid separation of what is syntactical and what is semantical."[110] In short, "if we talk as though an ordinary must be like an ideal language, we shall misrepresent the facts."[111] Along these same lines of argument, Katz has contended that the ideational theory is the best alternative available in the explanation of human communication.[112] Nor should we be too quick to forget that the conditions which Alston suggests as necessary and sufficient for the ideational theory are exactly those utilized in Searle's illocutionary paradigm ('promising') as we noted in Chapter I.

Finally, we need to take stock of the behavioral theory of meaning, or as it is occasionally called, the stimulus-response theory. The behavioral theory asserts that 'meaning', that is, the meaning of an utterance, is the stimuli that evoke it as an utterance and/or the responses that are in turn evoked. Whereas the logical test of the ideational theory was that two expressions have the same use if and only if they are associated with the same idea or ideas, the behavioral theory would hold that two expressions have the same use if and only if they are involved in the same stimulus-response connections. Such hypostatizations offer us a means for attempting the distinction of expressions, but very little is offered in the direction of a definition for 'meaning'. This difficulty is most apparent with the behavioral theory since meaning is a causal function of the similarity of stimulus behavior and/or response behavior in the use of language. One is apt to forget how simplistic this theory can be. To argue that a word or even a complete utterance is consistently associated with a given expressive or perceptive behavior is clearly contrary to common experience. Obviously, there are regularities of behavior, but they are hardly determinate. Nonetheless, Quine has argued with force that the behavioral theory of meaning is the best hope for disentangling philosophy from its fruitless attempts to explain problems, especially those of a metaphysical nature. He argues, in short, that the "questions of philosophy, when real at all, are questions

---

[110] J. L. Austin, *Philosophical Papers*, 2nd ed., ed. by J. O. Urmson and G. J. Warnock (London : Oxford University Press, 1970), p. 67.

[111] Ibid., p. 68.

[112] Katz, *The Philosophy of Language*, p. 176.

of language."[113] In summary, we should note that the same logical
issues that confront the ideational and referential theories are also
present here. That is, the same words can represent different behaviors
and at the same time different behaviors can be explained by the same
word.

We are left to account for the fact that persons do use utterances
and they do use them to communicate more or less successfully most
of the time. So that in spite of the logical difficulties with explaining the
'meaning' that is communicated, we are fairly certain that meaning
cannot be specified in a logical sense as a 'content' in any substantial
sense; at best, meaning seems to be a 'notion' in a conceptual sense.

1.2. *Natural Meaning*

Within the context of communication by speech acts, Austin notes
that "the difference between one named speech-act and another often
resides principally in a difference between the speech-situations envisaged
for their respective performances."[114] And indeed, this appears to be
exactly where our analysis is, having confronted the ideational, referential,
and behavioral theories of meaning. Each theory is formulated on
the basis of a speech situation envisaged to account for a particular
abstract version of language performance. As we shall see later on, the
very nature of the illocutionary act is founded on this perspective. Thus,
we are left with the question of meaning as a structure of relationship
that functions *as if* it were a state of affairs, a speech act content.

The use of the term 'natural' in connection with meaning derives in
a historical sense from the distinction between a 'natural sign' and a
'conventional sign'. In a primitive sense, a natural sign was taken to be
self-referring while a conventional sign was a human artefact. On a
more sophisticated level and with a contemporary perspective, a natural
sign is a historical artefact (phenomenalism) while a conventional sign
is a situational artefact (phenomenology) both of which are most
notably present in any natural language. In other words, the distinction
between natural and conventional is vaguely based on use.[115] This ambi-

---

[113] W. Quine, *Word and Object* (Cambridge, Massachusetts : The M.I.T. Press, 1964), p. 271.

[114] Austin, *Philosophical Papers*, p. 151.

[115] C. I. Lewis, "The Modes of Meaning" in *Semantics and the Philosophy of Language*, ed. by Leonard Linsky (Urbana : University of Illinois Press, 1952), pp. 50-63; see my *Speaking and Semiology* (The Hague and Paris : Mouton and Co., 1970).

guity can be resolved in the study of language by looking at the manner in which utterances are issued and the situation that results therefrom.

Grice argues that there are "under the head of natural senses of 'mean' such senses of 'mean' as may be exemplified in sentences of the pattern '*A* means (meant) *to do* so-and-so (by *x*), where *A* is a human agent."[116] Although such an account of meaning is accepted more or less without question,[117] it is fundamentally an account of linguistic meaning as being equivalent to the way language functions as a syntactic system. In other words, natural meaning is a view that semantics is a function of syntactics. Yet, "the danger in using grammatical processes to argue for aspects of meaning lies in using the same aspect of meaning to argue for the existence of the grammatical process in the first place."[118] And as Chomsky points out,

In fact, the notion 'representation of meaning' or 'semantic representation' is itself highly controversial. It is not clear at all that it is possible to distinguish sharply between the contribution of grammar to the determination of meaning, and the contribution of so-called 'pragmatic considerations', questions of fact and belief and context of utterance. It is perhaps worth mentioning that rather similar questions can be raised about the notion 'phonetic representation'. Although the latter is one of the best established and least controversial notions of linguistic theory, we can, nevertheless, raise the question whether or not it is a legitimate abstraction, whether a deeper understanding of the use of language might not show that factors that go beyond grammatical structure enter into the determination of perceptual representations and physical form in an inextricable fashion, and cannot be separated, without distortion from the formal rules that interpret surface structure as phonetic form.[119]

In short, it is conceptually restrictive to attempt to locate 'meaning' by an analysis which takes meaning to be a state of affairs in order that the process generating that state of affairs may be known. In short, "it ought to be the case that sentences that show formal reflexes of the speech act for which they are used, rather than of the speech act that their surface form seems to represent, will be those that are felt to mean what they *do* rather than what they say."[120] This is one issue that

[116] H. P. Grice, "Meaning" in *Philosophical Logic*, ed. by P. E. Strawson (London : Oxford University Press, 1967), p. 40.

[117] Some fundamental assumptions are tested by Hilary Putnam, "Meaning and Reference," *Journal of Philosophy* 70, no. 19 (November 8, 1973) : pp. 699-711.

[118] Sadock, *Toward a Linguistic Theory of Speech Acts*, p. 103.

[119] Noam Chomsky, "Form and Meaning in Natural Language" in *Communication : A Discussion at the Nobel Conference*, ed. by L. G. Augenstein (Amsterdam and London : North-Holland Publishing Co., 1969), p. 80.

[120] Ibid., p. 102.

Grice attempts to confront with his 'non-natural theory' of meaning as a different kind of speech act meaning, i.e. a shift from understanding the content of a speech act as constative to performative.

1.3. *Non-Natural Meaning*

Grice argues that in contrast to 'natural' meaning which describes what is *said*, 'non-natural' meaning is an account of what is *done*. As he suggests, "I include under the head of non-natural senses of 'mean' any senses of 'mean' found in sentences of the patterns '*A* means (meant) something by *x*' or '*A* means (meant) by *x* that ...'"[121] From this basic contention, Grice proceeds to offer the following generalizations of his theory :

(1) '*A* meant something by *x*' is (roughly) equivalent to '*A* intended the utterance of *x* to produce some effect in an audience by means of the recognition of this intention'; and we may add that to ask what *A* meant is to ask for a specification of the intended effect (though, of course, it may not always be possible to get a straight answer involving a 'that' clause, for example, 'a belief that ...').

(2) '*x* meant something' is (roughly) equivalent to 'Somebody meant something by *x*'.

(3) '*x* means $_{NN}$ (timeless) that so-and-so' might as a first shot be equated with some statement or disjunction of statements about what 'people' (vague) intend (with qualifications about 'recognition') to effect by *x*.[122]

In essence, the theory of non-natural meaning is an account of human communication in its most obvious form. This is to say, Grice is providing an *intentional theory of meaning* that is grounded in the description of meaning as the *effect* intended to be produced in a hearer by a speaker by recognition of the speaker's purpose in attempting communication. An example of this theory was presented in the first chapter of this study in Searle's account of 'promising'. There is still a serious question about the nature of the 'effect' produced, but that is an issue that will be taken up later.

---

[121] Grice, "Meaning", p. 40.

[122] Ibid., p. 46. These generalizations initiated a dialogue on non-natural meaning that lead to some refinement in the statement of the theory, but not any fundamental changes. See H. P. Grice, "Utter's Meaning, Sentence-Meaning, and Word-Meaning" in *The Philosophy of Language*, ed. by J. F. Searle (London : Oxford University Press, 1971), pp. 54-70; H. P. Grice, "Utter's Meaning and Intentions," *Philosophical Review* 78 (April, 1969) : pp. 147-177; and, Paul Ziff, "On H. P. Grice's Account of Meaning," *Analysis* 28, no. 1 (October, 1967) : pp. 1-9.

A result of the non-natural theory of meaning in terms of speech act analysis is the formulation of a general theory of human communication by Searle. As he argues in *Speech Acts* :

In speaking I attempt to communicate certain things to my hearer by getting him to recognize my intention to communicate just those things. I achieve the intended effect on the hearer by getting him to recognize my intention to achieve that effect, and as soon as the hearer recognizes what it is my intention to achieve, it is in general achieved. He understands what I am saying as soon as he recognizes my intention in uttering what I utter as an intention to say that thing.[123]

Searle does amend this account somewhat by suggesting that Grice's theory of meaning is "defective" in two critical ways. First, Searle argues that Grice's account does not take note of the extent to which meaning can be a matter of rules or conventions. "This account of meaning does not show the connection between one's meaning something by what one says, and what that which one says actually means in the language."[124] And second, the definition of meaning in terms of 'effect' confuses the illocutionary act resultant, 'force', with the perlocutionary act resultant, 'effect'. The answer to this objection lies in part with the concept of 'intention'. I would like to suggest that 'intention' is a term accepted by theorists like Searle and Grice as self-evident when it in fact has at least two special interpretations that are fundamental to the idea of speech act content.

To take up the question of 'intention' is to necessarily move into a discussion of the illocutionary act as such. The illocutionary act lies somewhere between the locutionary act of merely saying something and the perlocutionary of causing an effect in your listener. In the discussion of illocutionary acts, then, the ability to distinguish utterance 'force' and 'effect' should allow us to indicate the way in which 'intention' and 'intentionality' are fundamentally different in the speech act.

2. ILLOCUTIONARY ACTS

Austin's original distinction among speech acts was that a locutionary act contains 'meaning', while an illocutionary act has a certain 'force' in saying something, and a perlocutionary act achieves a given 'effect' by being uttered.[125] We have already discussed the nature of the locu-

---

[123] Searle, *Speech Acts*, p. 43.
[124] Ibid. Recall that Chomsky questions whether this is possible at all.
[125] Austin, *How to Do Things with Words*, pp. 99-101.

tionary act and its species, the phonetic, phatic, and rhetic acts. There are difficulties in distinguishing these acts from the illocutionary act inasmuch as the 'force' of an utterance appears to have characteristics which are not an exclusive function of the sentence uttered. As Ziff warns,

Semantic regularities are not simply regularities pertaining exclusively to linguistic elements : they include but are not restricted to such regularities. Semantic regularities are regularities of some sort to be found in connection with the corpus pertaining to both linguistic elements and other things, e.g. to utterances and situations, or to phrases and persons, as well as to utterances and utterances.[126]

However, Austin was quite aware of the difficulties involved. He recognized that "in general the locutionary act as much as the illocutionary is an abstraction only : every genuine speech act is both."[127] In this connection, Searle has argued that the locutionary-illocutionary distinction collapses even when one takes account of the locutionary species acts (phonetic, phatic, and rhetic).[128]

Searle contends that under close analysis one can only distinguish (1) phonetic acts, (2) phatic acts, (3) propositional acts, and (4) illocutionary acts. His analysis runs something like this. In any illocutionary act we must take account of the point or purpose of the act (for example, the difference between a question and a statement), the relative status of the speaker and hearer (for example, the difference between a command and a request), the degree of commitment undertaken (for example, the difference between an expression of intent and a promise), the conversational placing and role of the act (for example, the difference between a reply to what someone has said and an objection to what he has said.)[129] In effect, Searle is contending that illocutionary meaning as indicated by phatic and phonetic acts accounts for the meaning of sentences *per se*. But utterances are more than just *sentences*, they are *performances* and on this account the rhetic and illocutionary acts are without distinction in any major way. However, Searle introduces the idea of a 'propositional act' to describe the performative element (force) that is present in certain speech acts, over and above the meaning of

[126] Ziff, *Semantic Analysis*, p. 27.

[127] Austin, *How to Do Things with Words*, p. 146.

[128] John R. Searle, "Austin on Locutionary and Illocutionary Acts" in *Essays on J. L. Austin*, ed. by Sir Isaiah Berlin, *et al.* (Oxford : At the Clarendon Press, 1973), pp. 141-159.

[129] Ibid.

sentences. In short, propositional acts are abstractions which count as speech act contents in the same way that meanings represent sentence (linguistic act) contents. The fundamental nature of a propositional act is bound up with the notion of non-natural meaning, viz. the 'intention' present in the speech act.

2.1. *Intention*

Warnock was the first to characterize the force of illocutionary acts as the distinguishing feature that is 'extra-linguistic'.[130] This of course follows the direction that Austin himself suggested by characterizing illocutionary acts as performances in which "the effect amounts to bringing about the understanding of the meaning and of the force of the locution. So the performance of an illocutionary act involves the securing of *uptake*."[131] As Forguson suggests, then, to perform an illocutionary act a speaker must at least (1) perform a locutionary act (phonetic and phatic acts), (2) intend this act in the circumstances to have 'force', (3) secure uptake, and (4) in some cases, satisfy certain additional 'practice-defining' conventions.[132]

Since the securing of uptake specifies in a very explicit sense that the force of an illocutionary act is bound to a communication situation, we are of necessity moved in the direction of an analysis of how 'force', 'meaning', and 'intention' are related.

Austin argues that the perlocution or perlocutionary act is the result of saying something that "will often, or even normally, produce certain consequential effects upon the feelings, thought, or actions of the audience, or of the speaker, or of other persons : and it may be done with the design, intention, or purpose of producing them...."[133] We are to assume with Austin that the illocutionary act by contrast with the perlocutionary does not involve an 'effect'. 'Force' is something different. This distinction we will take up in a moment also, but presently we need to compare Austin's use of the terms 'intention' and 'effect'. In the discussion of illocutionary acts, he suggests the following examples : (1) "He urged (or advised, ordered, etc.) me to shoot her,"[134]

---

[130] G. J. Warnock, "Some Types of Performative Utterance" in *Essays on J. L. Austin*, p. 73.

[131] Austin, *How to Do Things with Words*, p. 116.

[132] L. W. Forguson, "Locutionary and Illocutionary Acts" in *Essays on J. L. Austin*, p. 170.

[133] Austin, *How to Do Things with Words*, p. 101.

[134] Ibid.

and (2) "He protested against my doing it."[135] Can we seriously take Austin's recommendation that these utterances are not intended to have an effect on the audience? As Campbell argues, this is too extreme a position to take.[136] Rather, one must argue, as Grice and Searle do, that there is an illocutionary effect, but one that is distinct from the perlocutionary effect (a consequence).

The illocutionary effect or force, I want to suggest, is nothing more than Austin's concept of 'uptake'. In the *perlocutionary act* the result of communication is an effect on the part of the listener as a consequence of the speaker's utterance. That effect is a response (verbal) or reaction (non-verbal); it is the *completion* of a situation. By contrast, the illocutionary act is the *alteration of a situation*. A speaker's utterance is simply recognized by the listener as an action that, when successful, transforms a situation of subjectivity (there is no relationship between the speaker and listener) into one of intersubjectivity (there is the relationship of 'having communicated' i.e., recognition of the force of the utterance). As Searle summarized the matter,

Human communication has some extraordinary properties, not shared by most other kinds of human behavior. One of the most extraordinary is this : If I am trying to tell someone something, then (assuming certain conditions are satisfied) as soon as he recognizes that I am trying to tell him something and exactly what it is I am trying to tell him, I have succeeded in telling it to him. Furthermore, unless he recognizes that I am trying to tell him something and what I am trying to tell him, I do not fully succeed in telling it to him.[137]

In simple terms, the illocutionary-perlocutionary distinction is one of degree rather than kind. The illocutionary force and the perlocutionary effect are not different kinds of 'effect'. They are different degrees of situational involvement for the speaker and listener moving from the alteration to the completion of a situation, i.e. from 'uptake' to response, this being an illustration of what Alston refers to as the 'illocutionary-act potential'.[138] In this connection, I believe that Whately is correct in his assessment that "testimony is of various kinds; and may possess various degrees of force, not only in reference to its own intrinsic character, but in reference also to the kind of conclusion that it is brought to support."[139]

---

135 Ibid., p. 102.
136 Campbell, "Locutionary, Illocutionary, and Perlocutionary Acts." p. 288.
137 Searle, *Speech Acts*, p. 47.
138 Alston, *Philosophy of Language*, p. 37 ff.
139 Richard Whately, *Elements of Rhetoric*, ed. by Douglas Ehninger and David

Put another way, (1) illocutionary force or (2) perlocutionary effect
is a difference in a communication situation (1) where the intention of
the speaker is understood (perceived description) by the listener (force)
or (2) where the intention of the speaker can be recognized (perceived
explanation) by the listener (effect). Here, I make an Austin-like distinction that Searle and others do not, viz. that understanding is knowledge
"in and by" a situation whereas recognition is judgment "of" a situation.
This is the distinction that Kant draws between 'conviction' and 'persuasion' which we will detail later on in the discussion of rhetorical acts.[140]
In any event, it is fairly clear that the understanding or recognition of
the speaker's 'intent' is the primary explanation for what illocutionary
force and perlocutionary effect are for the listener. At this juncture,
we can proceed to examine *how* intention is understood or recognized
as force or effect.

2.2. *Force and Effect*

In his discussion aimed at distinguishing the constative from the performative, Austin argues that "precision in language makes it clearer
what is being said — its *meaning* : explicitness, in our sense, makes
clearer the *force* of the utterance, or how ... it is to be taken."[141] Meth-
odologically, this demarcation between 'meaning' and 'force' is the same
that we have been making between description and explanation, and
which Searle has incorporated as his distinction between propositional
acts and illocutionary acts. The category distinctions involved here are
an expression of what Austin referred to as the Doctrine of Illocutionary
Forces.[142] Specifically the doctrine contrasts the descriptive with the
explanatory in the use of speech acts, for the illocutionary act is the
"performance of an act *in* saying something as opposed to performance
of an act *of* saying something."[143] Simply put, this is the contrast
between how something is said as a means of altering the situation,
as opposed to what is said as a method for specifying (describing) a
situation to which response or reaction can be appropriate.

Potter (Carbondale : Southern Illinois University Press, 1963), p. 58. First published
in 1828. (Whately was a tutor at Oriel College, Oxford from 1811 to 1822, then principal of St. Alban's Hall from 1825 to 1831.)

[140] Immanuel Kant, *Critique of Pure Reason*, ed. by Norman Kemp Smith (New
York : St. Martin's Press, 1929), p. 645 ff. First published 1781.

[141] Austin, *How to Do Things with Words*, p. 73.

[142] Ibid., p. 99.

[143] Ibid.

One of the major difficulties in comparing force and effect is the more or less unchallenged assumption that a statement or utterance in one case (i.e. one speech act) was illocutionary and that to be perlocutionary a second utterance is required (i.e. one speech act plus another speech act in response). This view is challenged principally by Hare who argues that speech acts have what he calls the 'phrastic' and 'neustic' elements.[144] As Heal summarizes the theory :

Any part of a sentence which refers or predicates or contributes towards the expression of a proposition is part of the phrastic. The business of the phrastic is to describe, represent or specify a state of affairs. By contrast, no neustic refers or predicates or expresses a proposition; the neustic has no descriptive role. Its business is to make clear (or help to make clear) the *force* (sometimes called "illocutionary force") of the utterance. It can do this because the utterance of a sentence containing the neustic *is*, and can clearly be seen to be, the performance of an action with a certain force.[145]

In short, the phrastic-neustic distinction is a method for arguing, as Heal does, that explicit performative utterances are indeed statements. The focus of this approach lies in the fact that an explanation is attempted for the performance nature of utterances within the traditional limits of description, i.e. what statements are. As a description it is not seriously effective, however, there are consequences at issue here which reflect on the nature of truth and statement. But, they are beyond the scope of this study. Suffice it to say that Hare further specifies the phrastic by inventing a new category, the 'tropic', to distinguish assertion (whose content can be negative) and affirmation as mood indicators in utterances.[146]

Austin attempts to come to grips with the force-effect distinction, and in so doing he suggests that on the basis of illocutionary force certain classes of utterances can be found. These classes are, respectively : (1) Verdictives, (2) Exercitives, (3) Commissives, (4) Behabitives, and (5) Expositives.[147] The first category of utterances, verdictives, are "typified by the giving of a verdict, as the name implies, by a jury, arbitrator, or umpire." It is important to note that Austin specifies

[144] R. M. Hare, *The Language of Morals* (New York : Oxford University Press, 1968), pp. 18 ff. and 188 ff.

[145] Jane Heal, "Explicit Performative Utterances and Statements," *Philosophical Quarterly* 24, no. 95 (April, 1974), p. 107.

[146] R. M. Hare, "Meaning and Speech Acts," *Philosophical Review* 79 (January, 1970), pp. 3-24, esp. 21. G. J. Warnock, "Hare on Meaning and Speech Acts," *Philosophical Review* 80, no. 1 (January, 1971), pp. 80-84, has suggested the ways in which Hare's analysis is of only marginal interest to the nature of illocutionary force.

[147] Austin, *How to Do Things with Words*, p. 150 ff.

that "they need not be final," that they can be like an estimate, reckoning or appraisal where a finding is given as to the fact or value in a situation, which for various reasons it is hard to be certain about. This qualification is a substantial clue to the fact that force alters a situation, without creating a new situation (effect).

Exercitives, as the name implies also, "are the exercising of powers, rights, or influence." Common examples of such exercitives are appointing, voting, urging, warning, and the like. Again, it is clear that such an act communicates a change in situation rather than the beginning of another situation. A listener may in fact respond, say, to a warning and thereby perceive the speech act as perlocutionary, but that is to describe the speech act as perceived and as belonging to the listener (effect, not force).

The third type of utterance is the commissive. They are "typified by promising or otherwise undertaking; they *commit* you to doing something, but include also declarations or announcements of intention, which are not promises, and also rather vague things which we may call espousals, as for example, siding with." It is with commissives that we can see most clearly that force and intention are closely linked. As with all illocutionary acts, the force of the utterance indicates the intention of the speaker, i.e. *how* the utterance is to be understood. By specifying how an utterance is to be understood, an explanation is given. In short, the force of an utterance is explanatory, while its meaning is descriptive. From the point of view of communication theory, an illocutionary utterance provides the listener with a linguistic act of description (language) with a simultaneous indication of the speaker's intention (speech). Taken together the illocutionary act as language-speech is the specification of a situation, i.e. a process that creates a state of affairs — but one which is subject to alteration. This is to say, a 'state of affairs' as a moment-to-moment construction, or, as a situation in flux. Put another way, and the way that Searle attempts to move, the utterance is an empirical linguistic item; it is a sentence that may take many forms, yet express the same proposition.[148] The proposition must be conceived as a 'propositional act' since the linguistic act in an utterance is meaning as intention, but in a special relationship which goes beyond Searle's analysis. The relationship is one of explanation rather than description. By focusing on 'propositional act' as *what* is communicated, instead of the 'intentionality' (how), Searle fails to discover that force

---

[148] Searle, *Speech Acts*, p. 22ff.

is essentially the communication of intention as a metacommunication item rather than a communication item. The distinction is critical, since the Grice-Searle account of meaning as the exchange recognition of intentions is open to the criticism of infinite regress, a problem that Lewis argues has psychological limits, but not logical ones.[149] We will take up Austin's notion of marking and metacommunication in the next chapter.

Austin's fourth class of illocutionary utterances displaying force are behabitives, to which he adds the editorial : "a shocker this." They are as he says a "miscellaneous group" having to do with attitudes and social behavior. Some examples are apologizing, congratulating, commending, condoling, cursing, and challenging. The element of force with behabitives appears to fall into the category of 'affective' or 'emotive' meaning which is so often distinguished from factual or 'cognitive' meaning. Indeed, Austin has the idea that is so typically experienced in social behavior, namely, the need to say something that on its face *means* very little as a description, yet is the very explanation that suggests the *force* of our feeling or appreciation for a person in a given situation. We quite literally attempt to alter the situation, but do not effect a category change in the condition of our speaker-listener relationship.

Finally in Austin's classification we have expositives which he says are difficult to define. "They make plain how our utterances fit into the course of an argument or conversation, how we are using words, or, in general, are expository." As examples he suggests utterances like : 'I reply', 'I argue', 'I concede', 'I illustrate', 'I assume', and 'I postulate'. We see in these examples a clear egocentric use of utterances that affect situations by constituting them as explicit forms of communication. Each example is also an illustration of a speaker altering a situation by his action almost irrespective of the listener, but not exclusively so, for their force depends on their being understood. As with the other utterance types, the propositional nature of speech act seems to be its distinguishing feature and is the issue that Searle discusses as a key element.

2.3. *Propositional Acts*

Before moving to a direct discussion of propositional acts as they are contained in speech act utterances, it will be helpful to note that the

---

[149] Lewis, *Conventions*, p. 83ff and 130ff.

distinction which we have been drawing in this study between description and explanation has its expression in the nature of propositions *per se*. As Searle points out :

We need to distinguish, as Frege failed to do, the sense of a referring expression from the proposition communicated by its utterance. The sense of such an expression is given by the descriptive general terms contained in or implied by that expression; but in many cases the sense of the expression is not by itself sufficient to communicate a proposition, rather the utterance of the expression *in a certain context* communicates the proposition. Thus, for example, in an utterance of "the man" the only descriptive content carried by the *expression* is given by the simple term "man," but if the reference is consummated the speaker must have communicated a uniquely existential proposition (or fact), e.g., "There is one and only one man on the speaker's left by the window in the field of vision of the speaker and the hearer." By thus distinguishing the sense of an expression from the proposition communicated by its utterance we are enabled to see how two utterances of the same expression with the same sense can refer to two different objects. "The man" can be used to refer to many men, but it is not thereby homonymous.[150]

In short, Searle provides a basis for the description-explanation distinction we have been employing as a means of distinguishing force, (the sense of an expression) and effect (the proposition communicated) in communication. The communication situation is the key element for this distinction and explains a key feature of intersubjective utterances, viz. "One can represent without communicating but one cannot communicate without representation."[151] This is not a new analysis, but is an important one for distinguishing the basis upon which Austin was led to conceive of the force-effect distinction. The original analysis was made by Russell :

Is it certain that we cannot have an image of *A* followed by an image of *B*, and proceed to *believe* this sequence? And cannot this *be* the belief that *A* precedes *B*? I see no reason why this should not be the case. When, for example, I image a person speaking a sentence, or when, for that matter, I actually hear him speak it, there does not seem, as a question of empirical fact, to be any moment at which the whole sentence is present to imagination or sense, and yet, in whatever may be the usual meaning of the phrase, I can 'apprehend the sentence as a whole'. I hear the words in order, but never the whole sentence at once; yet I apprehend the sentence as a whole, in the sense that it produces upon me the intended effect, whatever that may be.[152]

---

[150] Searle, *Speech Acts*, pp. 92-93; see p. 171.

[151] Searle, "Meaning, Communication, and Representation," p. 7.

[152] Bertrand Russell, "On Propositions : What They are and How They Mean" in *Logic and Knowledge : Essays 1901-1950*, ed. by Robert C. Marsh (London : George Allen and Unwin, Ltd., 1956), p. 318. Cf. Howard Pospesel, "The Nonexistence of Propositions," *Monist* 53, no. 2 (April, 1969), pp. 280-292.

The 'intended effect' is the 'force' of the illocutionary act, the understanding of what the words in the sentence mean and the explanation that the whole sentence, the utterance, offers. It is precisely this sequence of understanding that accounts for the 'propositional act'. As Searle argues, "The expression of a proposition is a propositional act, not an illocutionary act" because "one cannot just express a proposition while doing nothing else and have thereby performed a complete speech act."[153]

The question we are left with is this : What is the relationship in the meaning and force of propositional acts where intention is the basis of communication? Searle's answer, in another context but nonetheless appropriate, is that "the hypothesis suggested by the argument so far is that different kinds of illocutionary acts, in so far as they have propositional content, can be regarded as different modes in which utterances represent reality : an assertive mode, an imperative mode, a commissive mode, etc."[154] In point of fact, Searle suggests on the basis of propositional content that illocutionary acts are divisible into five basic types : (1) Assertives, (2) Directives, (3) Commissives, (4) Expressives, and (5) Declarations.[155] Let us look at each of these briefly and then compare them to Austin's Verdictives, Exercitives, Commissives, Behabitives, and Expositives. (In the description that follows I am quoting Searle directly.)

(1) *Assertives*. The defining point or purpose of the members of the assertive class is to commit the speaker (in varying degrees) to something's being the case, to the truth of the expressed proposition. All of the members of this class are assessable on the dimension of assessment which includes "true" and "false". This class includes *inter alia* statements, assertions, explanations, descriptions and characterizations. All the members of this class have the word-to-world direction of fit.

(2) *Directives*. The defining illocutionary point of these consists in the fact that they are attempts (of varying degrees) by the speaker to get the hearer to do something. Examples of this class are orders, commands, requests, prayers, entreaties, invitations, pleadings and implorings.

(3) *Commissives*. The defining illocutionary point of a commissive is to commit the speaker (again in varying degrees) to some future

---

[153] Searle, *Speech Acts*, p. 29.
[154] Searle, "Meaning, Communication and Representation," p. 14.
[155] Ibid., p. 15. Although I have not seen it, a more detailed account will be forthcoming as "A Classification of Illocutionary Acts" in Gunderson (ed.) *Minnesota Studies in the Philosophy of Science* Vol. VI.

course of action. Examples of commissives are promises, vows, threats, pledges, contracts, bets and guarantees. Both directives and commissives have the world-to-word direction to fit.

(4) *Expressives.* The defining illocutionary point of this class is to express the psychological state specified in the sincerity condition about a state of affairs specified in the propositional content. The paradigm expressives are thanks, congratulations, apologies, condolences, welcomes, greetings and applause. In general, they have no direction to fit.

(5) *Declarations.* It is the defining characteristic of this class that the successful performance of one of its members bring about the correspondence between the propositional content and reality. Successful performance guarantees that the propositional content corresponds to the world. Examples are declaring war, pronouncing someone man and wife, adjourning a meeting, excommunicating, christening, appointing, resigning and nominating. It is a general feature of Declarations that they require an extralinguistic institution for their performance. They have both directions to fit.

Even a brief review of Austin's *"families* of related and overlapping speech acts"[156] in comparison to Searle's "illocutionary act types" suggests that the categories are parallel. The difference is that Searle is attempting to specify via the proposition the difference between 'representation' and 'communication'. It is a difference which we have been analyzing all along, namely the description-explanation distinction. Searle would like to argue that the illocutionary act types carry with them propositions which are expressed in words and, because the uttering of the words are performance, explanations of the relationship between the word and the reality to which it refers. This latter point is Alexander's theory of communication, i.e. a speaker and listener are linked together in a situation by their mutual understanding and recognition of the proposition where that proposition is a synergism of symbol, referent, behavior, and concept. As Searle summarizes the point, as soon as a hearer "recognizes a communication intention (that is, the intention that he should know a meaning intention) he will know the meaning intention, hence communication is derivative from meaning and not conversely."[157]

We are left with a fundamental question which is how to specify the communication intention. Thus far in our analysis of speech act

---

[156] Austin, *How to Do Things with Words*, p. 149.
[157] Searle, "Meaning, Communication, and Representation," p. 20.

structures and speech act contents, we have located what Searle refers to as the meaning intention. The function of meaning and force as intention in the illocutionary act have suggested an account of propositional acts, but not in their use which constitutes a situation that is open to change. That is, we have examined the communication situation in its mode as an illocutionary act that alters the situation but does not have a consequence in the situational context. The only consequences in a 'force' sense are those which are egocentric for the speaker and/or listener. It is just this feature that Searle was hinting at in his systematic reference to the relationship between the word and the world in each of his illocutionary act types. The relational link in each case is through the perceiving speaker or listener. This structure (intentionality) while generated from an implicit infrastructure (force) in the illocutionary act is an explicit infrastructure (effect) in the perlocutionary act, which is the subject of the next chapter.

CHAPTER IV

SPEECH ACT COMMUNICATION

Austin in his Harvard Lectures discovered what he calls the 'performative'. We have come at this notion linguistically as a structural item and as a matter of content in use. Our analysis thus far suggests that of the original category distinctions between locutionary, illocutionary, and perlocutionary acts, we are left with a questionable distinction between the illocutionary and the perlocutionary. The illocutionary act is an utterance whose performance carries a certain 'force' which suggests that it functions to alter situations. Whereas, the perlocutionary act is a performance that carries a given 'effect' which evokes a change in the situation. The essential problem seems to be in the definition of the 'situation'. In the illocutionary act we have a situation that contains action and absorbs a modification. While in the case of the perlocutionary act we find a situation followed by another, yet causally related, situation. In short, the illocutionary situation is one of amendment, whereas that of the perlocutionary situation is one of addendum.

Before moving to a direct analysis of the perlocutionary act, it will be helpful to review the situational nature of performative speech acts as Austin conceived them.

There must exist an accepted conventional procedure having a certain conventional *effect*, that procedure to include the uttering of certain words by certain persons in certain circumstances, and further, the particular persons and circumstances in a given case must be appropriate for the invocation of the particular procedure invoked. The procedure must be executed by all participants both correctly and completely. Where, as often, the procedure is designed for us by persons having certain thoughts or feelings, or for the inauguration of certain *consequential conduct on the part* of any participant, then a person participating in and so invoking the procedure must in fact have those thoughts or feelings, and the participants must intend so to conduct themselves, and further must actually so conduct themselves subsequently.[158] (Italics mine).

[158] Austin, *How to Do Things with Words*, pp. 14-15.

In this description it is clear that Austin is attempting to cover all the factors that will explain both the illocutionary and the perlocutionary acts. On the other hand, it is less obvious how the illocutionary act factor of 'force' can be distinguished from its perlocutionary counterpart 'effect'. It is difficult, for example, to see how the utterance of the speech act at a bare minimum would not by its very doing affect the speaker, for surely uttering is a drastic change of situation from silence and can be counted as at least a subjective effect on the person in the situation. Well, this question leads us to examine in some detail the nature of the perlocutionary act.

1. PERLOCUTIONARY ACTS

The perlocutionary act for Austin is a speech act in which "saying something will often, or even normally, produce certain consequential effects upon the feelings, thoughts, or actions of the audience, or of the speaker, or of other persons : and it may be done with the design, intention, or purpose of producing them..."[159] In short, we have an act that may be accomplished intentionally or unintentionally as a consequence of utterance. Here we come upon a distinction that Austin surely was aware of, but did not specify in the precise way that he wanted. It is as Ayer contends "the technical way of describing verbs of this kind, which was introduced, I believe by Brentano, (which) is to say that they are intentional. There are some transitive verbs, like the verbs 'to eat' or 'to kill', which logically imply the reality of their accusatives; there can be no eating or killing unless there really are things that are eaten or killed."[160] In other words, we have to make a distinction between 'intention' as an analytic description of 'purpose' and 'intentionality' as a phenomenological explanation of 'consciousness'.

1.1. *Intention and Intentionality*

Up to this chapter in the study, we have been dealing with meaning according to the Grice-Searle formulation as the mutual recognition of an intention by a speaker and listener. That is, the speech act is an utterance which displays the purpose of the speaker and which has meaning because the listener recognizes that purpose. In specific terms

[159] Ibid., p. 101.
[160] Ayer, *Metaphysics and Common Senses*, p. 40.

of the illocutionary act, 'intention' is further specified as the meaning (i.e. purpose recognition) with 'effect' all of which is Austin's requirement that "a person participating in and so invoking the procedure must in fact have those thoughts or feelings, and the participants must intend so to conduct themselves, and further must actually so conduct themselves subsequently." Yet as Campbell comments, "all speech acts produce some effect upon the feelings, thoughts, or actions of those involved in such acts, and, therefore, *all speech acts are perlocutions.*"[161]

The difficulty with this analysis that attempts to move from meaning as intention to an explanation of force and effect is the confusion of speech act structure (purpose) with content (consciousness). I believe that this confusion can be illustrated by reformulating the usual definition of illocutionary act meaning. Searle offers this summary of the standard definition :

(1) The intention to produce a certain illocutionary effect in the hearer;
(2) The intention to produce this effect by getting the hearer to recognize the intention to produce the effect;
(3) The intention to produce the recognition by means of the hearer's knowledge of the rules governing the sentence.[162]

This description can become explanatory by reformulating the second and third criteria this way :

(1) The intention to produce this effect by the speaker recognizing and getting the hearer to recognize the possibility of this effect by its utterance as opposed to the utterance of other possibilities.
(Here 'intention' is properly 'intentionality' since consciousness of what constitutes the situation, i.e. a specific utterance as communication, rather than purpose, provides the basis for detecting purpose in the first instance. In other words, intention as purpose is a structure explained by intentionality, i.e. intention as consciousness, as an infrastructure.)
(2) The intention to produce the recognition by means of the speaker's and hearer's mutual knowledge and experiences of the conventions governing communication.
(The metacommunication condition of mutual knowledge is expressed here, since it is the hearer's knowledge of the rules governing sentences as well as the knowledge that the speaker is using these rules as self-reflexive to the utterance that accounts for understanding the utterance as one possibility among many and as the one appropriately belonging to the speaker's purpose).

[161] Campbell, "A Rhetorical View of Locutionary, Illocutionary, and Perlocutionary Acts," p. 290.
[162] Searle, "Meaning, Communication, and Representation," p. 2; *Speech Acts,* pp. 49-50.

This account is a direct shift from analytic method to phenomenological method which is necessitated by the inability of the logical account to escape an infinite regress of intention recognition which is an epistemological fault rather than an ontological one. Such a regress occurs because speaker and hearer actions are assumed to be identical, namely, to identify speaker purpose. In fact, the speaker function is to specify a purpose in communicating, but the hearer function is to specify justification in communicating. This is to say, that a speaker's utterance is purposeful from his point of view, but it is not for the hearer. In fact, the hearer would be at a total loss to recognize the purpose of the speaker if the hearer did not assume the utterance as a constituent element of his own consciousness. If anything, the utterance provokes the hearer's recognition of his purpose in listening, not because he knows the rules of sentence use, but because he knows the justification he can have for speaking in the way the speaker is performing. However, we are getting into matters that are the subject of Chapter V. For the present we need to turn back to the question of how intention and effect in the perlocutionary act are related.

1.2. *Effect*

Ayer reminds us that "What my neighbor sees as green may be very different from what I see as green; I cannot get into his mind to tell nor he into mine; but at least his usage corresponds with mine. We cannot communicate the content of our experiences, but we can at least determine that they have the same structure."[163] It is in this very sense that Searle argues that "the study of the meaning of sentences and the study of speech acts are not two different studies but the same study from two points of view."[164] In both Searle and Ayer, the assumption is being made that meaning is somehow 'in' the speaker and for a listener to comprehend it, a second, but similar category, meaning content must be in the listener. Where this is the case, we can say that there is a 'same' structure involved. What this analysis fails to take account of is that the 'same structure' is a notion assumed on the basis of the assumption of the speaker and the listener having *the same* intent or purpose.

Roughly, the analysis given above amounts to saying something like the fact that if a person uses a declarative sentence and a hearer

---

[163] Ayer, *Metaphysics and Common Sense*, p. 24.
[164] Searle, "Human Communication Theory and the Philosophy of Language : Some Remarks," p. 124.

recognizes it as the same, then the hearer perceives the 'intent' to inform. The listener may be even more certain because of the particular verb used, such as the speaker saying "I want to *inform* you of your rights." Such a *sentence* does just this, but the same phenomenon as an *utterance* does something quite different. Because the object of consciousness for the utterance is not available to the listener (he does not have the speaker's mind), the listener must supply his own content, i.e. the intent he *would have* if he were making the utterance in the role of speaker in the same situation. Thus, the parallelism in 'intent' as an account of meaning specifies not the similarity of sentence knowledge (use rules for language) but the comparison of states of consciousness. We have at this point a confusion of referents stimulated by our carelessness in not distinguishing communication rules from metacommunication rules, or more specifically, rules for sentence use from rules for utterance use. The referent in the *use of a sentence*, as Searle correctly points out, is the sentence : this is the basis for the non-natural account of meaning. Yet, the *referent of an utterance* is a state of consciousness. Here we must be clear to recall that a sentence is an abstraction from an utterance; it is an idea or concept about performance which is an item of behavior in human experience. In short, Searle is incorrect to argue that the meaning of sentences and speech acts are two views of the same problem.

Ayer's judgment is equally misleading. In a straightforward sense the content of our experiences cannot be communicated where we presume that our experiences are exclusively states of consciousness as mental entities of awareness. This assumption is not entirely the case. Any state of consciousness is a *consciousness of something*. Whatever that something is, it can be abstracted into sentence expression. This conclusion is, however, a very narrow view since we are thereby confined to saying with Searle that the state of consciousness of the sentence is involved rather than what the sentence represents. Rather, we must say that whatever that state of consciousness is, it (along with being abstracted into a sentence) can become the referent for a situation. This is to argue, that the communication exchange whether verbal or non-verbal or both constitutes as a performance event a given referent which is respectively for the speaker and listener their state of consciousness, their 'intentionality'. It is in this sense that perlocutionary acts always result in a consequential effect. As Austin notes :

It is characteristic of perlocutionary acts that the response achieved, or the sequel, can be achieved additionally or entirely by non-locutionary means : thus intimidation may be achieved by waving a stick or pointing a gun. Even in the cases of convincing, persuading, getting to obey and getting to believe, we may achieve the response non-verbally. However, this alone is not enough to distinguish illocutionary acts, since we can for example warn or order or appoint or give or protest or apologize by non-verbal means and these are illocutionary acts. Thus, we may cock a snook or hurl a tomato by way of protest.[165]

What we have then is not a means for distinguishing sentence type since the illocutionary and perlocutionary can have the same class of effect ('force' and 'effect' are synonymous), rather we have a means for distinguishing 'speaking' as a communication process and 'speech acts' as a communication representing a state of affairs. Speaking is generally a state of consciousness as expressed whereas the speech act is correspondingly a state of consciousness as perceived. When one abstracts these two phenomena and asserts them to be represented (which is a purely symbolic effort) by the same sentence token, then one ends up with an 'utterance' which from a linguistic point of view resembles the abstraction of a speaker's language use (the illocutionary act) or resembles the abstraction of a listener's (perception of) language use (the perlocutionary act). Thus, the illocutionary and perlocutionary acts appear to be distinct because they are different sorts of abstraction, yet they are indistinguishable since they abstract in the same way. In a very explicit sense, the Searle brand of speech act analysis confuses its methodology with its subject content. That is, analysis is a rule govern-ed *form* of behavior, but speaking (in its widest sense as communication) is a *function* of behavior (i.e. a way of behaving). In other words, Searle's analysis may contribute to our knowledge of how acts generally are generated, but not how situations come to be (conventional effect), nor how speaking and listening function as communication (real effect). This point can be clarified to a certain degree by contrasting the nature of 'arguments' and 'propositions'.

1.3. *Proposition and Argument*

The distinction that I want to make between arguments and propositions is succinctly put by Geach:

When I use the term "proposition", as I did just now, I mean a form of words in which something is propounded, put forward for consideration; it is surely clear that what is put forward is neither *ipso facto* asserted nor gets altered in content by being asserted. Unfortunately, this use of 'proposition', formerly

---

[165] Austin, *How to Do Things with Words*, pp. 117-118.

a well-established one, has become liable to be misconstrued, for the word has been appropriated by certain theorists for a supposed realm of timeless abstract 'intentional' objects, whose principle of individuation has thus far eluded capture in any clearly formulable criterion.[166]

As a preface to the discussion of the issue at hand, we need to recall that Searle very candidly suggests that "I do not know how to *prove* that linguistic communication essentially involves acts but I can think of *arguments* with which one might attempt to convince someone who was skeptical."[167] In other words, the term 'proposition' as Geach is wanting to use it refers to a neutral phenomenon, i.e. a phenomenon whose existence is not a matter of proof but relies instead on speculative justifications, viz., arguments.

However, when the epistemological question is raised and one needs to inquire into the process by which a person comes to know this proposition, then, a problematic matter is confronted. If Geach means to suggest in a literal sense that a proposition is 'propounded', that is offered for consideration where purpose or intent is at issue, then certainly we have an *argument*. The argument may not call for a judgment of truth or falsity and may in consequence not be technically an assertion. Yet, an 'argument' as Searle calls it is more than a neutral expression and suffers in the same way that Geach recognizes that the substitutes 'sentence' and 'statement' do when they replace 'proposition'. As an abstraction, the concept the proposition as an argument can be questioned on the method of its evolution, i.e. how it was generated. This seems to be a common approach, but we then shift from a question of what the argument is to how the argument is to be used. This is precisely where the illocutionary-perlocutionary distinction was generated by Austin. Both speech act types have effects which are generated in a slightly different way, but that does not account for 'effect', that accounts for the methodology.

In Austin's case we then have an account of speech acts based on distinguishing verb examples — a grammatical method; in Searle's case we have an account of speech acts by distinguishing rules of use — a semantic account; and, in Sadock's case we have an account of speech acts by distinguishing phrase generation (transformations) — a pragmatic

---

[166] Peter Geach, "Assertion" in *Readings in the Philosophy of Language*, ed. by J. F. Rosenberg and C. Travis (Englewood Cliffs, New Jersey : Prentice-Hall, Inc., 1971), p. 250.

[167] John Searle, "What is a Speech Act?" in *Readings in the Philosophy of Language*, p. 615. (Emphasis mine.) See Berel Lang, "Space, Time, and Philosophical Style," *Critical Inquiry* 2, no. 2 (Winter, 1975) : 263-280.

account. As Thomas comments, "ordinary contexts always involve, I should say by definition, special concerns, special questions to be answered, special decisions to be reached; not an a priori inquiry into the conditions for settling questions of that sort in general."[168] In short, explanation as a methodology statement or account should be preceded by a description of the phenomena being analyzed. One cannot attempt to account for speaking as a rule governed form of behavior, until an account of speaking is given. As Austin was well aware, "yet still perhaps we are too prone to give these explanations in terms of 'the meaning of words'."[169] The result is fairly clear, "we are left with a theory of meaning that is totally nonexperiential, words and sentences mean what they mean, rather than the experiential view that my nods or your words mean what my and your experience allow them to mean. That theory, whatever else it may be, has, in my judgment, no relationship to communicative and rhetorical reality."[170]

The view of the proposition that I am offering is the same that Sprigge calls a "propositional attitude." A propositional attitude is an attitude directed toward a proposition; this is what I have called a state of consciousness. Here, "a proposition in the relevant sense must be something which one may believe to be the case, wish to be the case, intend to be the case, and so on."[171] As such, the expression of the proposition takes on the status of an argument, an utterance that must be acknowledged within a situation (ranging from understanding to belief) to be a communication of anything, to be an expression or perception of reality as experienced.

I am arguing that the expression of a speech act does commit the speaker to an argument in the way that Searle suggests.

In general, the notion of presupposition of a speech act is the notion of a condition on the felicitous performance of that speech act, and in this case, a condition on the performance of that speech is that the proposition should be true, however, it is not the point of the speech act to commit the speaker to that proposition's being true. The point of the speech act of e.g. apologizing is simply to express sorrow or regret about the state of affairs specified in the proposition. But the truth of the proposition is taken for granted, it is presupposed.[172]

[168] Sid B. Thomas, Jr., "Is the Appeal to Ordinary Usage Ever Relevant in Philosophical Argument?" *Monist* 48, no. 4 (October, 1964), 0p. 544.

[169] Austin, *How to Do Things with Words*, p. 100.

[170] Campbell, "A Rhetorical View of Locutionary, Illocutionary, and Perlocutionary Acts," p. 291.

[171] Sprigge, *Facts, Words and Beliefs*, p. 132.

[172] Searle, "Meaning, Communication, and Representation," p. 18.

It is equally obvious that in such conditions the proposition is an argument in a communication context where the speaker offers to the listener a proposition which must be 'true' or 'false' to experience, although it need not be so in a literal sense.

That is, because we characteristically use the word 'true' only when a proposition is already under consideration, and because a proposition is characteristically put under consideration by the performance of some such speech act as asserting, stating or hypothesizing — because of these two facts, calling something true will place us in a certain relation to that initial speech-act; a relation, e.g., of agreement or endorsement, and conversely in the case of 'not true' a relation of disagreement.[173]

We are in fact back to Austin's notion of *uptake*. What is required of the speech act (the illocutionary-perlocutionary distinction is no longer meaningful) is that it achieve 'communication'. As previously noted, this should be a communication ranging from mere understanding to complete belief. As Austin suggests, even in the case of 'misunderstanding' there is a communication since the point is that an audience does not *have* to understand, rather than the fact that they do not understand. That is, the listeners do not have to *take* the communication as meaningful, truthful, etc.[174] We can conclude with Schiffer, then, that "for communication to be possible it is not necessary that it be known what people will utter; what is essential is that it be known that if someone utters x (in such-and-such circumstances), then it will mean such-and-such." In short, "it is this distinction which allows for the possibility of x being a conventional means for communicating that p (or a conventional means of exchange) without there being a convention to utter x only when (or when) one means that p (or a convention to trade by exchanging tokens of type x)."[175]

2. SPEECH AS COMMUNICATION

The rather obvious problem that we are faced with for the moment is how to distinguish, if one can, the act and the action in speech which counts as communication. As Searle forthrightly acknowledges, "I want to give a list of conditions for the performance of a certain illocutionary act, which do not themselves mention the performance of any

---

[173] Searle, "Meaning and Speech Acts" in *Knowledge and Experience*, p. 37.
[174] Austin, *How to Do Things with Words*, p. 33.
[175] Schiffer, *Meaning*, p. 155.

illocutionary acts. I need to satisfy this condition in order to offer an explication of the notion of an illocutionary act in general, otherwise I should simply be showing the relation between different illocutionary acts."[176] That Searle has failed in this effort is demonstrated rather concisely by Shirley.[177] In short, the nature of the analysis of the speech act is to show how it relates to other speech acts and I take this to be an account of communication as a process, namely a description of how communication works, but not an explanation of what communication is. It is methodology where :

Assertions can be supported or questioned by references to concrete features of language which focus attention beyond individual introspections of experienced phenomena. This in no way implies a sort of empiricism wherein linguistic "facts" are weighed and inferred from in an objective manner. It implies rather, a methodology lying between an objectivism that systematically overlooks important features of reality and a subjectivism that provides no way of confirming its claims. A linguistic phenomenology views language, not as a copy, nor as a veil, but as a mediator of reality.[178]

Thus, we are in a position with Searle of having to admit that the explanation of speech acts is a showing of how one speech act relates to another. Austin was vaguely aware of this defect with his notion of 'marking' and Fotion's concept of 'master speech acts' also seems to confirm it as we shall see.

2.1. *Marking and Master Speech Acts*

Austin notes that there are communication situations where the action must be suited to the word, where language must be made to specify a situation apart from its semantic description of action. That is, "when we use the formula 'I define x as y' we have a transition to a performative utterance from suiting the action to the word. We might add, too, that there is likewise a transition from the use of words as what we may call markers, to performatives."[179] By way of example, Austin suggests that there is such a transition or 'marking' from the word 'END' to the

[176] Searle, "What is a Speech Act?" in *Readings in the Philosophy of Language*, p. 623.

[177] Edward Shirley, "The Impossibility of a Speech Act Theory of Meaning," *Philosophy and Rhetoric* 8, no. 2 (Spring, 1975) : 114-122.

[178] Jerry H. Gill, "Linguistic Phenomenology," *International Philosophical Quarterly* 13, no. 4 (December, 1973) : 549.

[179] Austin, *How to Do Things with Words*, p. 65. This phenomenon is generally referred to as a "proactive verbal cue" in the literature of psychology and sociology.

end of a novel; or, a transition from 'message ends' to the end of a wireless message.

I want to argue that all speech acts are perforce markings for which we use the ordinary expression 'communication'. Fotion's concept of master speech acts is an attempt to formulate in a precise way just what Austin had discovered. He argues that the master speech act is a use of content to control aspects of the content of a subsequent speech act, in whole or in part.

It should be noticed that what is controlled in the speech acts which follow the master speech act can be the whole of each of these speech acts, the formula portion or the content.
1. Mode of expression (e.g., talking rather than writing; this code rather than that one).
2. Manner of speaking or writing (e.g., loudly rather than softly; slowly rather than rapidly; prosaically rather than poetically).
3. Topic (e.g., topic A rather than B; this aspect of A rather than that one).
4. Nature of speech act (e.g., commanding rather than promising; describing rather than evaluating).

To this specification, Fotion also adds :

To be sure, in so far as master speech acts perform these dual functions of identification and assessment, master speech acts are no different from any other speech act.[180]

Although Fotion is the first to designate by analysis the utterance feature which counts as a master speech act, we should recall that Strawson deals with a very similar, if not the same concept, in his discussion of the 'act of communication'. As he argues :

The speaker, then, not only has the general authority on the subject of his intention that any agent has; he also has a motive, inseparable from the nature of his act, for making that intention clear. For he will not have secured understanding of the illocutionary force of his utterance, he will not have performed the act of communication he sets out to perform, unless his complex intention is grasped. Now clearly, for the enterprise to be possible at all, there must exist, or he must find, means of making the intention clear. If there exists any conventional linguistic means of doing so, the speaker has both a right to use, and a motive for using, those means. One such means, available sometimes, which comes very close to the employment of the explicit performative form, would be to attach, or subjoin to the substance of the message what looks like a force-elucidating *comment* on it which may or may not have the form of a self-ascription.

[180] N. Fotion, "Master Speech Acts," *Philosophical Quarterly* 21, no. 84 (July, 1971) : 234-235.

And like Fotion, Strawson draws this related conclusion :

Since it is part of the speaker's audience-directed intention to make clear the character of his utterance as, for example, a warning, and since the subjoined quasi-comment directly subserves this intention, it is better to view the case, appearance not withstanding, *not* as a case in which we have two utterances, one commenting on the other, but as a case of a single unitary speech act.[181]

If the logic is good for making the case that the master speech act while different in content is similar in structure, i.e. that the infrastructures (one speech act plus a second speech act) constitute one structure (the speech act as communication act), then why not say the same for all speech acts in a given situation? The message that is communicated between speaker and listener and the interaction that brings it about would be a 'speech act'. It is clear that the process so described is something like the Platonic 'maieutic' in which we may discriminate items of linguistic content, but in which the communication structure is a synergism not properly understood by division into constituent infrastructures.

The speech act is the dialogue which constitutes a situation. The content of the speech acts suggests their relationship as an ongoing structure and 'marks' the end of that situation, i.e. points out or marks what is the effect of the interpersonal performance as a consequence *of* being said (structure) and *in* being said (content). "Thus in so far as a speaker 'performs' the master speech act (and a hearer accepts it), he is *in one act* both requesting (or commanding) and, through the content of that same speech act, giving force in one fell swoop to what other utterances are to follow."[182] This is a straight description and explanation of how a speech act comes to be a communication act in defining a situation. In short, we have discovered that speech act content and structure are respectively and appropriately communication and metacommunication. But before we can take up a direct discussion of the communication-metacommunication relationship, we need to say a bit more about the implications of Austin's 'marking' as a means of specifying the end to be achieved in the performance of a speech act. Historically, such a discussion has been the study of 'rhetoric' in its classical sense as the examination of effective oral discourse.

---

[181] Strawson, *Logico-Linguistic Papers*, pp. 159-160.
[182] Fotion, "Master Speech Acts," p. 237. See N. G. Fotion, "Indicating Devices?" *Philosophy and Rhetoric* 8, no. 4 (Fall, 1975) : 230-237.

2.2. *Rhetorical Acts*

According to Aristotle, "rhetoric may be defined as the faculty of observing in any given case the available means of persuasion. This is not a function of any other art."[183] As Baird indicates, the original Aristotelian view of rhetoric as persuasion included the idea that oral discourse was the 'implementation' of the means of persuasion to affect decisions. That is, rhetoric serves as an examination of the "modes of effective communication."[184] In terms of our continuing analysis, rhetoric is the historical name that we would assign to Austin's notion of 'marking'. Because, marking is the use of speech which indicates the end to be achieved; it is a 'rhetorical act'.

The very nature of the speech act as a performance carries with it the implication that the performance itself has a purpose. The 'intentional theory of meaning' which has been a continuing focal point of our analysis is a discussion of a rhetorical act rather than merely a speech act. The rhetorical act is the speech act at that point in performance before 'uptake' is achieved. In other words, the rhetorical act contains the 'available means of persuasion' but persuasion is not an effect or does not achieve effect until the listener takes up the speech act as part of the maieutic process. "An act of speech, then, is a meaningful utterance; it is a response that a speaker makes to a communicative context, a context that is partly external to him, partly internal."[185]

We may specify the distinction between the 'rhetorical act' and the 'speech act' by utilizing another historical distinction, namely that between 'conviction' and 'persuasion'. Kant makes this distinction in the philosophic sense in which we are interested.

The holding of a thing to be true is an occurrence in our understanding which, though it may rest on objective grounds, also requires subjective causes in the mind of the individual who makes the judgment. If the judgment is valid for everyone, provided only he is in possession of reason, its ground is objectively sufficient, and the holding of it to be true is entitled *conviction*. If it has its ground only in the special character of the subject, it is entitled *persuasion*.

---

[183] Aristotle, *Rhetorica*, Vol. XI of *The Works of Aristotle*, ed. by Sir David Ross (Oxford : At the Clarendon Press, 1946-1966), 1355b.26. The logical basis for the 'rhetorical act' as a speech act is detailed in my "Enthymeme : The Rhetorical Species of Aristotle's Syllogism," *Southern Speech Communication Journal* 39 (Spring, 1974) : 207-222.

[184] A. Craig Baird, *Rhetoric : A Philosophical Inquiry* (New York : The Ronald Press Co., 1965), p. 7.

[185] Karl R. Wallace, *Understanding Discourse : The Speech Act and Rhetorical Action* (Baton Rouge : Louisiana State University Press, 1970), p. 71.

Therefore, we are led to conclude :

The touchstone whereby we decide whether our holding a thing to be true is conviction or mere persuasion is therefore external namely, the possibility of communicating it and of finding it to be valid for all human reason. [186]

In other words, 'conviction' is the name we would assign to the speech act in its fullest sense as the achievement of uptake where marking has occurred. On the other hand, 'persuasion' would be the rhetorical act in which there is uptake, but marking is not at all clear. Part of the traditional misunderstanding of these two concepts derives from Whately's discussion in which the definitions for 'conviction' and 'persuasion' are the exact reverse of the Kantian explanation.[187] The unfortunate consequence has been a historical development of concepts by philosophers and rhetoricians that is at cross-purposes. However, that is a matter of no direct relevance to the present study.

In summary, we are able to distinguish the speech act as belonging to the discourse process of conviction and the rhetorical act as a constituent of the persuasion process. The key factor is the nature of uptake in which marking is achieved (with conviction) or is ambiguous/not achieved (with persuasion). The marking feature in both cases is symptomatic of the nature of the discourse involved with respect to the distinction between content and structure. That is, the speech act in its modality as conviction represents a discourse content (communication) and a discourse structure (metacommunication). Here, the structure indicates the manner in which the content is to achieve uptake and, in addition, how that content will effect (as marking) any resulting discourse as both structure and content. This is the very concept that Merleau-Ponty discusses as the speaking word or speech-speaking (parole parlante).[188]

By contrast, the rhetorical act or speech act in its modality as persuasion represents a discourse content (communication) and a discourse structure

---

[186] Kant, *Critique of Pure Reason*, p. 645.

[187] Whately, *Elements of Rhetoric*, pp. 36ff and 175ff. This confusion is the subject of philosophic examination and correction in Chaim Perelman and L. Olbrechts-Tyteca, *The New Rhetoric : A Treatise on Argumentation*, trans. by J Wilkinson and P. Weaver (Notre Dame and London : University of Notre Dame Press, 1969), esp. pp. 26-31. First published in 1958 as *La Nouvelle Rhétorique : Traité de l'Argumentation*.

[188] Lanigan, *Speaking and Semiology*, p. 187ff. See my "Semiotic Expression and Perception : Merleau-Ponty's Phenomenology of Communication," *Philosophy Today* 14, no. 2 (Summer, 1970) : 79-88; and "Merleau-Ponty, Semiology, and the New Rhetoric," *Southern Speech Communication Journal* 40 (Winter, 1975) : 127-141.

dependent on content (infracommunication). With this species of discourse there is the suggestion of the nature of uptake and the potential for marking (something like Alston's illocutionary act potential). Again in parallel fashion, this type of speech act is what Merleau-Ponty has called the sedimented or spoken word (parole parlée).[189]

In other words, when we consider a given discourse we can locate a series of speech acts some of which will function as 'master speech acts' indicating the ways in which the discourse is to evolve; and, some will be rhetorical acts which have a potential to be master speech acts, yet are not *per se*. They are dependent on the listener, and, the nature of uptake and its form as reaction (non-verbal) or response (verbal). The latter of course has more 'potential' to achieve the maieutic result. Having made these distinctions between the speech act and the rhetorical act, we can now take up the metacommunication-infracommunication distinction.

2.3. *Metacommunication and Infracommunication : A Phenomenology*

We should begin the analysis of metacommunication and infracommunication by noting with Johnstone that "a phenomenology of the rhetorical transaction would begin by assuming that rhetoric has an ontological basis, that it is a necessary condition of human existence."[190] This is to suggest that while the conditions for describing and explaining communication are bound up in the content and structure of discourse, the philosophic justification for the description and explanation must move from the strictly epistemological questions to their ontological base.[191] Such an examination is undertaken by Natanson in the context of rhetoric as we just discussed it above.

There is a rhetoric of convincing and a rhetoric of persuading, strange as that formulation may sound to ears used to hearing rhetoric spoken of as the art of persuasion. What we mean by this distinction is this : the understanding of techniques involved in attempting to control others, to convince them of this or that, is at a distance from any concern with risking the self of either

---

[189] Ibid.

[190] Henry W. Johnston, Jr., "Some Trends in Rhetorical Theory" in *The Prospect of Rhetoric*, ed. L. F. Bitzer and E. Black (Englewood Cliffs, New Jersey : Prentice-Hall, 1971), p. 84.

[191] Richard Lanigan, "Merleau-Ponty on Signs in Existential Phenomenological Communication" in *Studies in Language and Linguistics 1972-73*, ed. by R. W. Ewton and J. Ornstein (El Paso, Texas: Texas Western Press), pp. 73-88. See "The Concept of Logos" in Martin Heidegger, *Being and Time*, trans. John Macquarrie and Edward Robinson (New York: Harper and Row, Publishers, 1962), p. 55ff.

speaker or listener. The issue is one of manipulation. In the case of persuasion, technique is bound to the very meaning of the self, and rhetoric becomes the inquiry into the structure of communication — the art of philosophically locating the speaker and listener and speaking and listening as features of a world.[192]

We may suggest that the discussion of 'technique' in the case of persuasion is not unlike the Grice-Searle account of 'meaning intention' and as we have previously analyzed it. Such 'meaning' is ultimately to come to depend upon the master speech act/rhetorical act distinction. This distinction is primarily structural in nature as Johnston indicates, although the content aspect of the speech act is very much present. As Hays maintains, "language has several functions, such as passing on information about the environment, expressing emotional states, and exerting social control. Still another function of language is self-modification — a metalinguistic function."[193] This thesis has been argued in extreme form by Jakobson who suggests that every speech act changes the entire system of the language being spoken.[194]

While an analysis like that of Jakobson may serve to indicate the metacommunication aspect of the speech act, we must keep in mind that there is a parallel infracommunication aspect that also modifies the language or communication system as a whole. Hays argues that the metacommunication factors divide into two species, what he calls 'explicit metacommunication' and 'implicit metacommunication'.[195] The former is a direct statement or description, what Austin would call a constative. The latter is a set of proposals about the form of interpersonal relations that persons generate in their communication with one another. This is what Austin has called marking and the movement to the performative utterance.

The point here is that Hays does not fall into the difficulties that Austin did, because Hays specified the discoverable distinctions as

[192] Maurice Natanson, "The Claims of Immediacy" in *Philosophy, Rhetoric and Argumentation*, ed. by M. Natanson and H. W. Johnston, Jr. (University Park : The Pennsylvania State University Press, 1965), pp. 18-17 Cf. John Stewart, "J. L. Austin's Speech Act Analysis" in *Philosophers on Rhetoric : Traditional and Emerging Views*, ed. by Donald G. Douglas (Skokie, Illinois : National Textbook Co., 1973), pp. 192-205.

[193] David G. Hays, "Language and Interpersonal Relationships," *Daedalus : Journal of the American Academy of Arts and Sciences* 102, no. 3 (Summer, 1973) : 214.

[194] Roman Jakobson, "Concluding Statement : Linguistics and Poetics" in *Style in Language*, ed. by Thomas A. Sebeok (Cambridge : The M.I.T. Press, 1960), pp. 350-377.

[195] Hays, *op. cit.*

aspects of the discourse situation. That is, the 'explicit' feature indicates that a speech act content has a relationship to other speech acts in the same dialogue (Fotion's master speech acts) which is the 'infrastructure' phenomenon. In addition, the 'implicit' feature indicates that a speech act structure is a relationship (i.e. a relationship of a relationship) which is the 'metacommunication' phenomenon. Such a distinction is a phenomenological one that which argues that speech act analysis is basically ontological in contradistinction to the epistemological hypothesis as represented, e.g., by Skinner : "Analysis of these activities, together with their effects upon the listener, leads us in the end to the role of verbal behavior in the problem of knowledge."[196]

The phenomenological method by its focus on ontology offers a method for discovering and explicating the signifying process that is at once perception (infracommunication) and expression (metacommunication). By proceeding through the phenomenological method of description, reduction and intentionality (Hermeneutic), one can ascertain the synergistic nature of immanent and transcendent discourse signs in their modalities as speech acts and rhetorical acts. The lived-experience of speaking constitutes for the person a personal history as self-identify and a public history as cultural commitment. The semiotic convergence of perception and expression is an intentional structuring process that becomes an explicit rhetoric when articulated as lived-phenomena. The overt manifestation, the 'meaning', of lived-experience emerges at two levels of speaking : authentic or primordial speech, and, empirical or sedimented speech.

Authentic speech (la parole) is the creation of a lived-experience, a *Lebenswelt*. But, empirical speech (la langue) is the re-enactment of primordiality, an essential manifestation of the *Weltanschauung*. Authentic and empirical speaking are themselves semiotic functions of each other. The existential (la parole) and the empirical (la langue) are the infrastructure that come to constitute discourse structure (le langage). The ontological (infracommunication) gives rise to the epistemological (metacommunication). In short, the analysis of speech acts cannot properly resolve itself as an epistemological question before the ontological foundations have been examined. Our speech act analysis in this study is therefore reduced to the hypothesis that "in life, the

---

[196] B. F. Skinner, *Verbal Behavior* (New York : Appleton-Century-Crofts, 1957), p. 11. Cf., E. M. Adams, "Linguistic Analysis and Epistemic Encounters," *Philosophy and Phenomenological Research* 34, no. 3 (March, 1974) : 404-414.

essence of consciousness is communication, where one cannot determine what is ours and what belongs to others. Our perception of others is a modification of ourselves."[197] The explication of this ontological thesis is the concern of the next chapter.

[197] Maurice Merleau-Ponty, *Consciousness and the Acquisition of Language*, trans. by H. J. Silverman (Evanston : Northwestern University Press, 1973), p. 49n. See Edward MacKinnon, "Language, Speech, and Speech-Acts," *Philosophy and Phenomenological Research* 34, no. 2 (December, 1973) : 224-238; Anthony Manser, "Austin's 'Linguistic Phenomenology'" in *Phenomenology and Philosophical Understanding*, ed. Edo Pivcevic (New York : Cambridge University Press, 1975), pp. 109-124.

CHAPTER V

EXISTENTIAL SPEECH AND THE PHENOMENOLOGY OF COMMUNICATION

The thematic question with which we started in the initial chapter of this study was that formulated by Searle, namely, "How do words relate to the world?" It is this question which led us to examine speech acts, their structure and content, and their performance or process nature in the constitution of 'communication' as a state of affairs. In short, we analyzed what language and speech seemed to be in view of how they are used in the ordinary discourse of common situations. In this chapter,[198] I wish to take the analysis one step further, and in a different direction, by examining how phenomena such as language and speech are constituted by a person who generates a 'world' of such phenomena. It is, if you will, the phenomenological explanation that necessarily follows from the analytic description of human communication.[199]

In his essay "A Plea for Excuses," J. L. Austin tells us "When we examine what we should say when, what words we should use in what situations, we are looking again not *merely* at words (or "meanings," whatever they may be) but also at the realities we use the words to talk about : we are using a sharpened awareness of words to sharpen our perception of, though not as the final arbiter of, the phenomena."[200]

---

[198] This chapter appears here for the first time, although previously scheduled as a monograph in the journal *The Human Context / Le Domaine humain.*

[199] Walter Cerf, "Critical Review of *How to Do Things with Words*" in *Symposium on J. L. Austin*, ed. by K. T. Fann (London : Routledge & Kegan Paul, 1969), 374-379; Paul Ricoeur, "Phenomenology of Freedom" in *Phenomenology and Philosophical Understanding*, ed. Edo Pivcevic (New York : Cambridge University Press, 1975), pp. 173-194.

[200] J. L. Austin, *Philosophical Papers*, 2nd ed., ed. by J. O. Urmson and G. J. Warnock (London : Oxford University Press, 1970), p. 108. "Everything which belongs to the species of exhibiting and explicating and which goes to make up the way of conceiving demanded by this research, is called 'phenomenological'." Martin Heidegger, *Being and Time*, trans. John Macquarrie and Edward Robinson (New York : Harper and Row, Publishers, 1962), p. 61.

Austin himself is insightful enough to tell his reader that this approach is not properly to be called linguistic or analytic philosophy, but linguistic phenomenology.[201] One is rather startled with the parallel conception that is expressed some three years earlier (1953) by Maurice Merleau-Ponty who argues that "the more energetic our intention to see the things themselves, the more the appearances by which they are expressed and the words by which we express them will be interposed between the things and us."[202]

In this chapter, then, I would like to suggest an original way of answering Searle's question, "How do words relate to the world?", which is a reply that embraces the epistemology of Austin's linguistic phenomenology. Indeed as Cerf notes, Austin's methodology is "tinted by a descriptive attitude made popular by phenomenology and by a holism in conflict with traditional English atomism and in harmony with existentialism from Heidegger to Merleau-Ponty."[203] The approach of existential phenomenology is very nicely described by Austin's phrase, a "sharpened awareness of words to sharpen our perception of phenomena." Or as Cerf summarizes :

To elucidate the total speech act in the total speech situation is more than, and different from, anything that goes by the name of logical or linguistic analysis. Elucidation is a relooking, a looking without blinkers, a seeing things freshly. And the things to be so viewed are not the things and facts that make up the universe, but the whole complex nexus of man doing things in the world by way of using words.[204]

In short, I would like to suggest in answer to Searle's question that a person's phenomenological existence generates communication at all semiotic levels and that this communication constitutes a lived world. I propose to elaborate this contention, first, by briefly orienting the analysis as existential, rather than transcendental, phenomenology. Second, I should like to look rather closely at the three modalities of encountering phenomenological existence in communication which accounts for the bulk of my analysis. Finally, I shall offer a few conclusions about the dialectic critique that this analysis attempts.[205]

---

[201] Ibid.

[202] Maurice Merleau-Ponty, *In Praise of Philosophy*, trans. by John Wild and James Edie (Evanston, Illinois : Northwestern University Press, 1973), p. 20. The nature and scope of Merleau-Ponty's phenomenology of communication is detailed in my *Speaking and Semiology* (The Hague and Paris : Mouton and Co., 1972).

[203] Cerf, "Critical Review," p. 352.

[204] Cerf, "Critical Review," pp. 370-371.

[205] One of the first methodological comparisons between Austin and Continental

1. EXISTENTIAL PHENOMENOLOGY

Existential phenomenology is a philosophic attitude and method of analysis which takes as its central concern a person's consciousness of living as his origin of being and as his history. As an attitude, existential phenomenology focuses upon the philosophic problem of the modalities of *consciousness* which are manifest as essential in the process of being a person, which is to say, the nature of personal existence. This is the problem of phenomenological existence. As a method, existential phenomenology utilizes a critique of living and lived *experience* which is the essence of being a person, of encountering other people, and of the history which they constitute by sharing and inhabiting a common world. This 'sharing' and 'inhabiting' involve the problem of communication and more specifically of 'communicative-intention'. In combining the existential attitude and the method of phenomenological critique I am following, in the tradition of Merleau-Ponty, the procedure of phenomenological description, phenomenological reduction or epoché, and hermeneutic. This is to say, the method is a description of phenomena as immediately given in consciousness, a reduction of the phenomena by ignoring their constitution in consciousness, and the determination of the sense or meaning of phenomena by discovering the structure that inheres in the presence to consciousness of phenomena (genetic experience).

I am deliberately posing the problems of phenomenological existence and communication in existential terms to avoid any misconception about the direction I wish to follow. While a great debt is owed to Edmund Husserl for his exacting examination of consciousness as 'pure' or transcendental phenomenology, his early writings from the *Logical Investigations* up to the *Cartesian Meditations* tend toward an unacceptable idealism in the attempt to make philosophy a socalled "rigorous science". In contrast, the approach represented by parts of the late Husserl and primarily in the subsequent additions and interpretations of Merleau-Ponty presupposes the necessity of making philosophy the proper objective of phenomenological inquiry. The existential approach correspondingly presumes the methodological necessity of making phenomenology ontological as an infrastructure

phenomenologists is John Stewart, "Revolutionary Aspects of Austin's Speech Act Analysis," unpublished paper presented at the Speech Communication Association Conference, Chicago, Illinois, (December, 1972).

to logic. In specific terms of the present study, the existential approach emphasizes a new way of looking at consciousness.

In Husserl, consciousness is the power of signification by constituting the distance and absence of things. For him, speech and perception are signified as one, as 'appearing' for a conscious perceiver. But, in Merleau-Ponty perception becomes the experiencial basis and genetic origin of all operations of consciousness. This consciousness signifies, judges, and speaks. The existence of the person and the sense of the existence of things are revealed simultaneously in perception. Consciousness in this view is the constituting appearance or experience of perception. Perception expresses consciousness, and in this sense phenomenological existence has its origin and extension in communication.

I propose to bring the attitude and method of existential phenomenology to bear upon three phenomena in which a person encounters his own existence and that of other persons and things. Such an analysis discloses, if I may paraphrase the Husserl of the *Cartesian Meditations*, the interrelation by which a person's experience of subjectivity constitutes the consciousness of intersubjectivity. The three phenomena or objects of conscious experience that I have in mind are (1) perception, (2) expression, and (3) communication. The examination of perception and expression reflects the subjectivity of persons whose intra-personal experience of *silence* and *thought* generates their self perception and whose experience of using *language* is constitutive of self expression. The third phenomenon, communication, reflects the intersubjectivity of persons whose mutual experience of *speaking* and *speech acts* are interpersonal synergisms of their subjective perceptions and expressions. This sketch of the relationships I want to deal with is analytically helpful, but conceptually misleading in its logical familiarity.

We must cut through, as it were, these usual and presumed categories of perception as only sensation in a causal sense, of expression as merely the utterance of sensible language, and of communication as the imparting of a message. Our critique should expose the interdependent modalities of the *living* and the *lived* in persons. Here, the term 'living' is simply a phenomenological label for genetic consciousness, while the word 'lived' refers to constitutive consciousness or experience. By way of illustrating my analysis I would like to use the word 'vertical' to describe the relational force of the phenomenological concept of *living*; similarly, the word 'horizontal' will be used to describe the term *lived*.

By 'vertical' I mean to imply 'existential' in the sense of active being here and now, namely, living. The vertical is a modality of being that is articulated in consciousness at three levels : (1) Silence, (2) Synchronic Language, by which I mean the current state of language use in a given society, and (3) Speaking. I want to stress that the three levels are synonymous in describing an active here and now presence of consciousness. By 'horizontal' I mean 'empirical' in the passive sense of being there and then, namely, lived. The horizontal is a modality of being that is manifest at three levels which I designate as (1) Thought, (2) Diachronic Language, by which I mean the institutional nature of language in a given culture, and (3) the Speech Act. These familiar terms are intended to emphasize the passive values that one encounters as synonymous experiences of there and then, as the absence of genetic consciousness.

The term 'living' has the experiencial force of an activity or situation occurring right now, what one is always conscious of as the present moment. Necessarily, the location of 'living' as the 'now' of human time carries with it the spatial implication of the vertical, of being positioned 'here'. Hence, 'vertical' appropriately suggests the active sense of here as the locus of possibility, as the origin of undetermined capability. On the other hand, the term 'lived' implies an experience of the event or activity which occurs then, in the past or future as the receding or approaching present. It is the experience of the past or future as a determinate reflection of the present. Correspondingly, the spatial implication of 'then' in the time continuum is a location which is always 'there'. Thus, the word 'horizontal' points to the passive sense of being a relational position, of being the location and fulfillment of an ability. In short, living or the vertical is how a person is existing, while the lived or the horizontal is how a person has existence.

To go a step further, vertical and horizontal as descriptions point to the relational direction or way of becoming that composes the respective experiences of existing and existence into one consciousness of being a person alive. The vertical experience is the consciousness that a person has of his own *presence*. In more familiar, but slightly misleading terminology, the vertical experience is the 'subjectivity' of a person in the sense of being the self that one is conscious of as himself. In contrast, the horizontal experience is an 'objectivity' in the sense of a person being the object or body which has existence and which is the *absence* of the self. The horizontal is one's own consciousness of himself which he constitutes by being a genetic self. Unlike the traditional dichotomies of the mind-body paradigm, the terms vertical and horizontal assume the implicit unity and reversibility of both modalities in being a person.

Just as the physical sensation of vertical and horizontal planes explains the occurrence of visual depth awareness, so the synergism of existing (the vertical) and existence (the horizontal) accounts for the intra-personal (unity) and interpersonal (reversibility) consciousness of being a person who generates and constitutes his own world in life.

It is helpful at this point to introduce the term 'other' as opposed to self. On the one hand, 'other' means 'another person' who is not oneself; a person whom one *experiences* as other than himself. This is the inter-personal sense of 'other' which correspondingly assumes that 'person' is the name of vertical existing. In contrast, the intra-personal sense of 'other' refers to one's own consciousness of being an *experiencing* person, what I call horizontal existence. In other words, the interpersonal sense of 'other' is another person generated in the consciousness of a person, while 'other' in the intra-personal sense is the person constituted in his own consciousness. In order to avoid using the term other in these two senses, I shall adopt the convention of using the term 'other' to refer only to another person. And, the word 'person' will refer to the person himself in conjunction with the terms 'consciousness' and 'experience' which are adequate to specify respectively the genetic and constitutive modalities of the person in either intra-personal or interpersonal rela-tionship.

The similarities of consciousness and experience as intrapersonal and interpersonal relationships naturally suggest that the problem of communication is synonymous with the problem of phenomenological existence. There are three themes which indicate philosophically how a person's consciousness and experience communicate phenomenological existence. First, the theme of phenomenological perception in which silence and thought are genetic and constitutive of consciousness in a person. This first theme discloses a person's consciousness of himself. Second, the theme of phenomenological expression by which the person experiences synchronic and diachronic language. This theme discloses experience as the object of consciousness for a person. Third, the theme of phenomenological communication which is the experience of being a conscious person and experiencing the consciousness of the 'other' through speaking and the speech act. This last theme discloses the meaning or sense of experience as the intentional object of a person's consciousness.

The first theme, perception, indicates the dialectical interaction between the vertical and horizontal modalities of being a person capable of intra-personally experiencing silence and thought as existence. Expression, as the second theme, suggests a person's vertical and horizontal modalities of being a person experiencing the normative and genetic language of his society, i.e., synchronic language, and the cultural value or constitutive nature of language as diachronic. Finally, the theme of communication recommends the synergism of perception and expression, that is, the dialectic movement of the vertical and horizontal in which speaking is genetic consciousness and the speech act is constitutive experience for the person and the other. In each of these themes the dialectic movement of consciousness and experience is a unity as vertical and a reversibility as horizontal which combine into one phenomenon. This experienced phenomenon is the person who is defined by (1) the living and lived experience, (2) the pre-conscious and conscious modes of consciousness, (3) the immanent and transcendent modes of experience, (4) the absence and presence of the object of consciousness in experiencing, and (5) the pre-reflective and reflective modes of consciousness.

The brevity of outlining the problems of phenomenological existence and communication from the various methodological perspectives of existential phenomenology has no doubt created a reasonable amount of ambiguity. I hope some clarity will be forthcoming in the detailed analysis to follow where each of the three themes is analyzed systematically in its vertical modality, then in its horizontal modality. Each modality is progressively put to a phenomenological description, reduction, and hermeneutic. This is followed by an analysis of the dialectic movement in the two modalities of each theme.

2. ENCOUNTERING PHENOMENOLOGICAL EXISTENCE

2.1. *Perception : The Becoming of Speech*

Perception is normally construed to be either the act of apprehending phenomena with the mind or through the organs of the physical senses. In both cases, the human agency is conceived to be an exclusively receptive object. The usual concern of the theorist or practitioner who studies perception is with *what* is taken into the human organism. In the present analysis, I wish to avoid the preconceptions posed by this naturalistic view of the person and concentrate on the phenomenological status of *how* the person is able to and does perceive, how perception is able to engage the person. Taking the vertical and horizontal structure of human existence as a point of departure, we can examine first the modality — *existing* — in which the person is the subject of self perception, and secondly, the modality of *existence* in which the person is an object of self perception. In this regard, *silence* is the name we can apply to the activity of self perception, i.e., consciousness of oneself. And, *thought* is the awareness that we attach to the process of self perception in which one is the object of his own experience.

2.1.1. *Silence.* As with each topic to follow, I would like to examine silence or the vertical modality of existing as progressively (1) a description of consciousness, (2) a reduction of the intentional object of consciousness, and (3) a hermeneutic of experience. At the descriptive level of consciousness it is possible for a person to engage his own awareness of living, that is, to discover how and in what way he is, not in *fact*, but in *process* existing. A person first discovers that by engaging in self perception he becomes an agent who can actively know and feel his own situation of being alive. This is to say, a person experiences the intra-personal perception of *self by self* as his ability to be conscious of himself as the agent of himself. Necessarily then, as we speak of a person knowing his own situation of living or feeling that he is alive, we mean there is a consciousness of the process of existing which is describable as the knowing and feeling. Yet, existing is more than the sum of intellection and sensation. There is in consciousness a synergism which makes consciousness more than its analytic constituents of mind and body in action. In this vertical modality, then, how a person perceives is to take himself as the subject of his consciousness. In so doing he discovers that the perception of self by self is properly a state of ability or capability that is not strictly a conscious or reflective activity by which we mean causal engagement of the mind. Rather, the perception of self by self is a *pre-conscious* engagement. Perception as pre-conscious is a possibility of existing, it is not a fact of existing. As a possibility of constituting experience, the pre-conscious is a person's living experience of existing. To put it another way, the possibility of the state or situation of existence is one modality of the existing process which engages a person as his being a person. Hence, the pre-conscious is a possibility of a person's consciousness, yet a possibility that is bound up with the ability to be engaged by the person.

In much of the present context of discussion, perception and its preconscious status are virtually synonymous with 'expression' inasmuch as the act of engaging perception is in large part the act of expressing. When a person engages self perception there is simultaneously the expression of self to self as the subject of perception. The pre-conscious status of perception as a possibility able to occur is dependent upon the person's expressive capability as a subject for himself. In order to be capable of being the subject of self perception the person must be capable, as a subject, of self expression. Thus, as the vertical phenomenon of existing perception and expression are not distinguishable to the person. Note that I have used the phrase "distinguishable *to*", not the words "distinguishable *by*" which indicates clearly that perception and expression are a possibility and capability for the person, not a fact of or determination of the person. In short, perception and expression are not objects experienced by some sort of detached self, rather they are the person as such.

A person whom we describe as perceiving and expressing himself at the pre-conscious level of experience is existing in an immanent modality of being. This is to say, the living experience of the person is describable as silence inasmuch as self perception and self expression generate the same, identical experience of a person as himself. But how is one to grasp this pre-conscious, immanence we call silence if it is truly pre-conscious, yet immanent to experience? The answer lies in the second step of the present analysis which is the reduction of the intentional object of consciousness or silence.

Silence, whose essence we describe as pre-consciousness and immanence, is necessarily an object of pre-reflective consciousness since its expressive and perceptive appearances are indistinguishable to the person himself. Hence, it is helpful to recall that our analysis is directed toward understanding how silence is a style of perception, not what silence is as an admixture of sensa. Because we are concerned with *how* rather than *what*, the pre-reflective object of consciousness as silence is not perception or expression, nor any mediating combination of the two which succumbs to the psychological model of concept formation in verbal and nonverbal behavior. Rather, the pre-conscious and immanent essence of silence is the *identity* of perception and expression for the person alone. Silence as this relationship is the immanent experience of the person who lives and is existing with the possibility in the pre-conscious, the possibility and capability of perceiving and expressing himself to himself. Yet, the possibility and capability are always immanent, given to the person without reflection, without the intervention of sensation. Hence, silence is an intentional object of consciousness which is no less than the intrasubjective perception-expression identity. Silence is one style of capability, the capability of finding meaning in oneself.

The sense of perception as silence is the third area of present interest, that is, the hermeneutic of a person's perceiving experience of himself. Perceiving is the pre-conscious act of the person when he takes himself as the subject of perception. Such perception is *manifest* immanently to the person alone and thus perceiving is uniquely an intra-personal dimension of meaning as existing. It is the living awareness of an "I" which is capable of self engagement as experience. This perceiving is the intra-subjective capability of being alive in an immanent manner by affirming the identity of self to self, that is, affirming the uniqueness of the person in existing as himself. It is the manifest singularity that identifies the person as a Body-subject. The consciousness of perceiving as so described is the vertical modality of existing experience which is, which means, an essential *absence*. The experience is the absence of any constitution as a reflective act, a fixed sensation, or a judgment. Silence or the perception of oneself as a subjectivity of person in expression is the becoming of speech. It is a style of becoming which is the ability to articulate a presence as the genetic embodiment of language and speech. In short, silence is the perceived absence of appearance, the absence of how a person *is*. Silence is the perception of how a person can be manifest to himself, how existing can be expressed to himself.

2.1.2. *Thought.* Perception as a horizontal modality of existence concerns itself with a person's self perception of himself as an objectivity. This notion is more explicit in the view that it is possible, if not just common sense, that a person can perceive himself as a self or appearing subject in contradistinction to himself as an object or material appearance. The most contemporary development of this idea is, of course, Martin Buber's "I-Thou" bifurcation which is a personal way of referring to the subject and object constitution of a person. However, I think it would be less confusing philosophically to rely on the ordinary language use of the pronouns 'I' and 'me' and also 'I' and 'you', rather than Buber's formulation. Obviously, the 'I-me' and 'I-you' relationships refer to the subjectivity of appearing and the objectivity of appearance for the person and the other. In such a conceptual framework, the objective mode of perception in which a person engages his own thought is the process of perceiving not 'myself', but 'oneself'. The person perceives the other in himself and this perception constitutes the other in himself, and, this perception constitutes the dimension of thought in the lived person. That is, perception as thought is the horizontal process by which the person monitors his subjectivity as a modality of his body and the objectivity of his body as a modality of his subjectivity. Thus, there is not subject and object proper, only the person as appearing subjectivity and objectivity in appearance. This is to say, the person as intra-subjectivity lives vertical being as silence and horizontal being as thought.

For the first time a person is aware of his experience that expression is the appearing object of his perception and that perception, likewise, is the appearing object of his expression. The discovery of perception and expression as the essence of a person's objectivity to himself is an explicit indication of conscious activity and appearance pursuant to personal existence. Perception and expression are conscious activities at the thought level and they require each other as their objective counter part in the agency of constituting existence for the person. In the present horizontal modality of existence perception can be described as a functioning transcendence in consciousness. This is to say, perception as thought is not a capability nor an ability which is immanent to the person in the process of existing, rather it is a fact that is constituted by the agency of existence. The significant consequence is the person's ability to distinguish perception and expression as different dimensions of his consciousness. Expression and perception are objective to the person as appearances of himself. The perceiving act of the person is dialectically immanent to himself and combines with expression as the transcendent agency of understanding. And conversely in thought, expressing is immanent with perception being the transcendent meaning.

Appropriately at the reductive level of analysis, it becomes clear that thought as the appearance of consciousness is a person's horizontal existence as a *reflective* objectivity. This is to say no more than the fact that perception and expression, not perceiving and expressing, display a dialectic power of *reversibility*. To put it more clearly, perception *translates* expression and vice versa for the person alone. Thought is the ordinary language term which designates for us the reflective object of a person's horizontal existence. When the person is in the process of perceiving himself, that is, self perception as an appearance, the experience of the object is the fact of self existence for the person. Such existence as a reflective state manifests the reversibility whereby the perception or expression of oneself is the object of experience which occurs as appearance for the existing person. In short, thought is the level of meaning by which a person perceives his objectivity and expresses his objectivity through self existence. The lived meaning of thought is precisely the becoming of speech as perception. As such, perception is the fixed modality of reversibility that is expression, the explicit meaning that can be manifest and articulated in language and speech as the appearance of thought. Such meaning is precisely the hermeneutic level of consciousness in existence and in the horizontal experience of consciousness.

Perception as thought is an intentional object of the passive process of existence. It is the passive concern of the person's consciousness which is manifest as an appearing object, which is nothing else but thought. Thought is the reflective product of a person's perception of himself as an appearance. At the hermeneutic level, thought is an intra-personal dimension of the person. Thought is the self or subjectivity which acknowledges oneself, that is, acknowledges the body or appearance of existing which is a person's existence as such. Thought explains to a person his possibility of being a person as a person. The person is no longer an isolated 'I' whose pre-consciousness is the solitary ego, rather the person reflects his objectivity as cogito. The person comes to understand the 'I' which lives the 'I', the transcendent realization that 'I' am 'myself'. The intra-personal awareness is the hermeneutic experience which explains the person's horizontal existence of *self for self* which is manifest as a lived *presence*. A person is conscious of himself as a Body-subject. The hermeneutic truth of this consciousness is its total possibility, yet passivity in meaning. The person's presence is known to himself as being *there* in appearance and not the presence of here which is the active pre-conscious. The reflective consciousness constitutes the person as there *then*. The primacy of perception as genetically now is not available because it is already lived experience, no longer living consciousness. The lived experience of thought becomes the only possible object of consciousness which is the constituting appearance of oneself as a person.

2.1.3. *The Dialectic Movement of Perception.* By way of explaining the dialectic movement of silence and thought in perception, I would like to first summarize the bifurcated relationship which constitutes equally a *unity* and a *reversibility* of the subjectivity and objectivity, or Body-subject, which is a person. In perception, the person is a vertical unity of experience which is pre-conscious and immanent in himself. Hence, the vertical unity is absent to the person as an object of reflective experience. Such an absence indicates the inadequacy of reflection as a specification of intra-personal experience which is immanent. The person so constituted as a subjectivity in the person is a pre-reflective appearance to himself. Put another way, a person is aware of his existing prior to his reflection on it.

The dialectic status of the person is preeminently a self defined unity of the consciousness of experience as becoming which is incapable of fixed existence. The experience which is intra-personally only preconscious as a unity is incapable of being present as such. The vertical person is an absence which is existing. Here the essential dialectic is the active and unified presentation of self to self, the here and now of existing which a person lives, knows, senses as silence. On the other hand, the person is a horizontal reversibility which is conscious and transcendent. The person has existence, the passive experience of being conscious of himself as being there and being then. The experience locates the person as an appearance to himself and as an object which is not immanent in himself. Rather, the object is transcendent to himself as the product of his reflection. The reversibility of horizontal existence is precisely the culmination of being the perceived-perceiver, of being the appearing object of experience which is there and as the object of consciousness which was then. By definition, then, the dialectic status of the person is a presence to himself which he is able to engage only through reflection. And, reflection is simply the self constituting reversibility of becoming by which the person achieves fixed existence and is present as such to himself. The horizontal modality of the person is a presence of himself as the appearance which he is conscious of as being objective in existence. The existence of himself transcends his existing. Thus, the essential dialectic is a reversible presentation of self for self. The expression and perception of the person are the object of himself and the object is no more than the appearing reflection of his own consciousness. In short, the person is always present to himself in thought. The existing person has existence as such in the perception of himself which is the intra-personal dialectic of silence and thought. The dialectic theme of perception is the unity and reversibility that generate the intra-subjective experience that a person has of his own consciousness of being in the world. Phenomenological perception is fundamentally a becoming of speech, that is, an articulation constituting intra-personal consciousness as experience.

2.2. *Expression : The Sediment of Speech*

In our common experience the meaning of expression generally includes any process or activity which reveals or indicates something about a person, event or thing. Expression is also conceived to be the polar opposite of perception when expression is broadly inclusive of conception and sensation alike. This is actually a brief way of noting that expression is often determined by a definition which relies heavily on the analogue of the physical transmission of sound — the so-called behavior of encoding selected symbolic material for explicit reception by a hearer. As in the case of perception, this naturalistic and technological conception of expression stems from an over fascination with *what* expression is, rather than the phenomenological concern with *how* it comes to generate itself as part of a person's experience of existence.

How a person engages in expression is a matter best examined from two perspectives : what I am calling synchronic and diachronic language which I take to be two aspects of the general institutional nature of interpersonal expression. In this respect, I take expression to include use of any semiotic system. In using the linguistic terms, 'synchronic' and 'diachronic', I intend a very modified and generalized use beyond their technical restriction in linguistics to rather specific features of language.

2.2.1. *Synchronic Language.* Every person is born into a language community and so as he matures in the use of this language certain normative features of his participation become constituted as part of his experience. It is this social experience of language that I want to designate as synchronic language. I do not intend that my idea of the social experience of language should be equated with the philosophic notion of 'institutional language', for I take the latter to be captured by my use of 'diachronic language'. Rather, the social experience of language is the phylogenetic expectation that a person has of how his language will express his meaning and himself.

At the descriptive level of consciousness, synchronic language is first of all a vertical mode of existing in which the person expresses his presence as a subjectivity to another person. This is to suggest that another person is able to perceive in a person's expression the fact that he is an existing subjectivity present as a subject of expression. Put another way, the existing person experiences the perception of himself by the other and what is perceived is the expression of the person. As an experience of language, the meaning of the person to the person is that of expressing *self to other*. In short, the experience of perception by the other person and expression by oneself is indistinguishable only by and to the other person. For the existing person, the experience of himself is mirrored in the experience of the other and, as such, is distinguishable to the person himself. The person who is the appearance of the other person is thereby constituted as a *pre-conscious* and *immanent* experience of himself.

The experience is pre-conscious because the appearance of the person as a subjectivity is apparent to the other person as the experience of subjectivity for himself. This vertical experience of synchronic language is immanent as such for the other person who is not able to distinguish it as the perception of expression of the person as himself. The other person necessarily perceives in a person's language the immanent experience that makes the articulation a distinct expression of personal perception.

At the second level of analysis synchronic language can be reduced to an intentional object of experience for the other person. As such synchronic language is pre-reflective as an object in a person's vertical modality of existing. For, the combination of a person's perception with his expression in the form of synchronic language is a dialectic unity having the force of an identity for the other person only. The expression and perception which a person lives in himself are manifest to the other person in language, yet the person himself is not able to distinguish his perception from his expression. Only the other person is able to separate the genetic experience which he perceives as constituting the subjectivity and objectivity of the person, that is, the person's conscious appearance.

There is a problem with synchronic language as a unity of perception and expression since the other person encounters a person's language in an active manner and makes it part of the person's modality of existing, but not a fact of his existence. On the other hand, the person himself experiences the passive reversibility of perception and expression in appearance. Yet, both persons can in using language reverse their interpersonal modalities of consciousness thus reconstituting their intrapersonal modality of experience. While this appears to be a point of contradiction, it is not, as Merleau-Ponty first noted. Such an ambiguity merely defines the reversible situation in which a negative element encounters another such element and yet the conjunction has a positive character. The ambiguity is simply the interplay of the vertical and horizontal modalities which simultaneously are genetic and constitutive. We misunderstand the dialectic in trying to locate a single modality for our analysis by imposing an analytic division on a phenomenological situation.

As a pre-reflective object for the person, synchronic language is — to use an anthropological metaphor — a sediment of speech as expressing.

This is to say, the experience a person has of expressing himself is the generation of a living meaning. It is a participation in language as interpersonal consciousness and experience of the other person. At this hermeneutic level, expressing is the consciousness of subjectivity through intersubjectivity. This is, to put it another way, the living experience of the phenomenological fact that 'I' generate the 'me' which is constituted as 'you' for the other person. A person's subjectivity is constituted in the intersubjectivity of the other person who also lives as a subjectivity (a 'me') within his own objectivity (a 'you') which is both himself (an 'I') and the person 'I' am (a 'me' as 'you'). This dialectic state of here and now is the active experience of the other person which constitutes an absence of the *other to other*. Put more precisely, the hermeneutic reflection teaches us that the living subjectivity of a person is the absence which is manifest to another person whose own subjectivity is generated as that absent objectivity. This is to say, for the existing person the 'I' is the mark of absence for 'me', yet it is manifest to another person as his existence, his 'me' (the first person's 'you') which in turn is his existing appearance as his 'I'.

2.2.2. *Diachronic Language.* Just as every person lives in a language community of other people that represents a certain state of social discourse, so each person is simultaneously experiencing the institutional force of language which is what I call 'diachronic language'. The institutional nature of diachronic language is precisely its cultural value as a context or situation traditionally used for interpretation. The diachronic norm is a measure of language now in comparison to language used previously — which is itself the possibility of language in future usage. Hence, the diachronic use of language captures the horizontal modality of existence in juxtaposition to synchronic language which encloses the vertical modality of existing. Diachronic language as a motif of existence indicates the expression of the person as an object to another person. As a description of consciousness the person embodied in his consciousness and perception is not distinguishable to the other person. The inability of the other to penetrate beyond the objectivity which is the person present to him is the conscious disclosure that the person exists as an appearance to him. The person's perception is simply consciousness of self by self and expression is no less than the experience of self to self. The person is fundamentally incapable of distinguishing himself from the object present to the other. Hence, the person knows himself as the other knows him, that is, as an appearance. As such the person is *pre-conscious* in his own experience which is also *transcendent* to his consciousness. This is to say, the person is pre-conscious inasmuch as he is able to be the reflective object only for the other person. The person in his subjectivity is thereby transcendent in his objectivity to the other person.

The experience of diachronic language is reducible to a person's consciousness of the intentional object in which language forms the reflective object of the other person. Diachronic language is such a reflective object insofar as the other person is able to perceive it as the expression of a person's objectivity in general for others. Hence, the intentional object is reflective by force of the dialectic reversibility which the other person experiences in the process of his perception which is the *translation* of a person's expression. Conversely, the other person's expression is a translation of the person's manifest perception.

The level of meaning for diachronic language, therefore, is the reversibility of experience which the other brings to bear upon the perception of self by self and the expression of self to self that is the objectivity present to the other. The lived meaning of this modality of existence in diachronic language is a sediment of speech which is the experience of *expression*. Not expressing, but the passive process which is expectation for the other as only expression. In short, expression is the person manifest as object to the other person. Obviously, the manifestation is language itself, yet language with its diachronic value of being there and then by its appearing reference. This hermeneutic level of experience for expression as diachronic language is an *interpersonal* dimension. It is through the necessary constitution of the other person that a person is an object to himself. In other words, the hermeneutic of expression is the experience by the other person of the objectivity of the person. The other's consciousness is an appearance of a 'myself' which is pre-reflectively the 'I' that is the person himself. In short, the experience of expression is the other person's consciousness of the objectivity itself, that is, of the person's appearance as other. This consciousness of the *other for other* is the *presence* of the object of a person himself and the object of the other person. The objective presence is precisely the person's appearance there and then as a person.

2.2.3. *The Dialectic Movement of Expression.* Synchronic and diachronic language are the dialectical poles of expression which are manifest constituents of a person's vertical experience of existing or his horizontal

experience of existence. Synchronic language is pre-conscious and immanent experience, hence indicative of a person's pre-reflective consciousness of the identity inherently generated in the perception and expression
of oneself as a person. This pre-reflective object which is synchronic
language constitutes the subjectivity of a person for another person.
That is, language in its synchronic disposition articulates the subjectivity
of a person to another person therein constituting the interpersonal
level of meaning. The dialectic dimension of meaning at the interpersonal
level is the living experience which presents the subject of personal
experience as the objectivity which is the absence lived by another person.
That is, the subjectivity of one person is taken as the dialectic completion of another person by uniting the first person's subjectivity with
the second person's objectivity. The dialectic of expression, then, is in
one perspective the union of what is vertical appearance in one person
with what is horizontal appearance in another. Such is the vertical
dialectic of existing in expression as synchronic language. The dialectic
movement allows for the emergence of the person from among
other people as an expressing consciousness able to be experienced by
others.

At the diachronic level of language, the person is an object to the
other person. The person in his subjectivity is necessarily pre-conscious
and transcendent, thus a reflective object of a person's consciousness.
The reflective object is generated by the reversibility of perception and
expression of the subjective person as appearing to the other person.
This is another way of saying that the level of meaning in diachronic
language is the reversibility of perception and expression which translate
one another for the other person alone. As such, meaning is a sediment
of speech as an appearance that is fixed in expression by being the object
perceptible to another person, yet constitutive of the very person who
expresses to the other. The dialectic meaning is thus the expressing of
oneself to another in one's subjectivity by the objectivity of meaning
which alone can be expressive.

The hermeneutic experience of expression then comes to be strictly
interpersonal and constitutive of a person's other for the other, or
objectivity for another subjectivity. This is to say, the objectivity of the
person who is present to the other person is present as an other person
from himself. That is, he is present in appearance and present as an
objective other to his own living subjectivity. Expression is, therefore,
the horizontal existence of a person as the passive object of appearing
to another person. Expression is the force of diachronic language as the

sediment of speech, as the meaning or sense posited there and then in consciousness.

2.3. *Communication : The Being of Speech*

Phenomenological existence as a living experience is embodied in the phenomena of human communication as the dialectic of *speaking* and *speech acts*. This is to say, the vertical or genetic experience of speaking and the horizontal or constitutive experience of speech acts together constitute communication. And, it is a person's consciousness of living and the lived in direct relation to other persons. As such, communication comes to constitute the history which is a person and his consciousness of other's experience.

2.3.1. *Speaking.* A person's vertical modality of existing in communication is the experience of speaking. This uttering experience is the modality of existing in which the person lives as a subjectivity to himself, yet is also a subjectivity for the other person as well. This relationship of a person and another person through one subjectivity means that in perception the encounter of a person by another is the same encounter that the person has with himself. Likewise, in expression the subjectivity which expresses the person is also the subjectivity which is expressive to the other person. Perception and expression in this dimension are only distinguishable by and to the other person. The other is able to separate the perceiving subject from the experience of subjectivity in the person, while the person himself apprehends only his subjectivity, but not his separate appearances as perception and expression. For the person, then, the experiences of perception and expression as speaking are *pre-conscious* and *immanent*. Speaking is pre-conscious because it is only appearance, the probable and possible experience to be lived, yet not distinguishable to the person in the vertical modality of his living. And, speaking is immanent because it is given to the person as such. Speaking is contingent on the other person for meaning as a living experience, yet it thereby constitutes the ground of conscious meaning for the person.

Speaking thus comes to constitute a *pre-reflective* object of a person's consciousness; it is properly the intentional object of the reduction to consciousness. For the articulating person expression is perception and conversely within the intentional object. Speaking is the identity of appearance that the person lives and which the other can recognize as being lived in the person. The expressing appearance generates expression and the perceiving appearance generates perception whereby both appearances constitute an identity of consciousness of oneself and the other.

The level of meaning which characterizes speaking is a living meaning in contradistinction to lived meaning. Speaking is the being of speech which generates the experience of *communicating*. The experience is active and determining of the process surrounding the person as his consciousness of self engagement among others. Put another way, speaking is a person communicating wherein that communicating manifests the sense of self existence which can only be called *a person existing*. At this hermeneutic level of analysis, the communicating act of speaking is an intra-personal definition of existing; it is the vertical being and consciousness as one person. Speaking means no less than the phenomenological truth that a person lives the articulated reality that is 'I' and 'me'. In speaking there is no arbitrary distinction between the 'I' and 'me' which properly constitutes the vertical modality of being a person. There is only the consciousness of a person being absent to himself, that is, the genetic consciousness that is not yet constituted as experience. The absence is the consciousness of the active force of speaking, of encountering oneself here and now. There is no possibility of being an object to oneself as one might be to another person, for in that case one would be the object person — the constituting speech act that is available to the other as well as to oneself. This absence as the consciousness of speaking is the experience of *self to self* which has no presence, no objectivity to oneself. In this sense, existing as manifest in speaking is an objective absence to the person. For the person, speaking is simply consciousness of living in a particular style which is communicating.

2.3.2. *Speech Acts.* Communication, as opposed to communicating, is the horizontal modality of existence which is the experience of the speech act by which a person is himself the object of meaning and the meaning to the other person. At the descriptive level of phenomenological analysis, the speech act enables a person to perceive the other person. This is to say, the speech act allows the person to experience his own objectivity in the same way that the other person does. The corresponding situation exists for expression in which the person expresses his objectivity as the other person would express the first person's objectivity. In short, perception and expression of the person as the speech act are the generation of an object as the person and it is this same object which is present to the other person.

Necessarily, the speech act dimensions of perception and expression are distinguishable by and to the person alone. Only he is able to distinguish the objectivity which he is for himself and the objectivity which he is for the other. In other words, the essence of the speech act experience is *conscious* and *transcendent* to the person alone. Only the person experiences his own objectivity as consciousness and yet that consciousness is transcendent as an experienceable object for the other person. The speech act is a conscious experience of appearance which carries the horizontal modality of existence as accessible to the person and the other alike. Also, the speech act is transcendent inasmuch as the object of consciousness, the speech act experience itself, is for the person and the other the mutual existence which completes the individual existing by constituting it.

The speech act in this developing context is a *reflective* object of consciousness, as was alluded previously, because it is the constituted product of the person and the other in the process of *translating* perception into expression and vice versa. The speech act is the reflective act of translation of experience into consciousness and consciousness back into experience. This translation process is a dialectic movement that has a meaning value as the *reversibility* of perception and expression which constitutes the object. That is, the speech act is mutually constitutive in use by the person and others. This lived meaning which is shared in the speech act is the being of speech which is *communication*. Communication is not the subjectivity of consciousness, but the objectivity which contains the passive modality of existence. Communication is the fixed experience whose hermeneutic designation is *interpersonal* meaning; it is encounter by exchange for people. Communication is the realization and lived experience of recognition that the speech act as such is the reversible experience which teaches the person that 'I' am a 'you' for the other person. This is to suggest that the person experiences in communication the *presence* of his *self for the other*. The speech act as communication is the objectivity lived by the person as an appearance of objectivity available to the other person. The speech act is the horizontal relationship between a person and another which is lived, which is the passive consciousness of appearance located there and then. It is the fixed object of experience that was previously the living experience of speaking. The speech act is the passive being of speech communication which is the horizontal modality of existence.

2.3.3. *The Dialectic Movement of Communication.* The vertical and horizontal modalities of communication which I have labelled 'speaking' and the 'speech act' reflect two dimensions of experience for the person and others. As a subjectivity the person is essentially pre-conscious and immanent in his experience of being. His speaking generates a pre-reflective object of consciousness for himself and the other person. The speaking experience constitutes the being of speech which is manifest in the active process of communicating. The communicating process is thereby an identity of perception and expression that is available to the person and the other. It is an active process of the intra-personal realization of the existing consciousness of self to self. That is, the active experience which is the awareness that 'I' am 'me' and that neither dimension is distinguishable from the other for another person. Hence, speaking is the vertical modality of existing that is always a subjectivity to oneself and always an absence of the available objectivity in appearance that the other experiences of one as a person.

In the objectivity dimension of being a person, communication is manifest as the speech act. Such an act is essentially conscious and transcendent for the person and for other persons. The speech act constitutes a conscious experience because it is the reflective objectivity of a person's experiences as constituted by the reversibility of one's perception and expression. The speech act is in fact the translation that interacts between perception and expression for oneself and the other alike. Put another way, the speech act is the passive process of communication that is properly interpersonal experience or meaning. The mutual exchange of the person with another person is the existence of self for the other. The exchange is the encounter of one's presence which is lived as the horizontal mode of existence. The encounter is between the reflecting consciousness and the experience of oneself which is there and then in constitution. The passive person that one sees as the objectivity of himself and which others also experience as such is a meaning constituted in the speech act. Communication is thus the objectivity manifest in the opposition between the communicating person and others in the dialectic subjectivity of phenomenological existence.

3. THE DIALECTIC CRITIQUE

The present phenomenological analysis yields several conclusions about the nature of existence in relation to communication. However, the fundamental ground of phenomenological existence and communication revealed by the analysis is the synergism which is captured in both and which is definitive of both. First, there is the synergism of the vertical and the horizontal modalities of existence. Second, there is the synoptic style present in the vertical mode alone. And third, there is thy synoptic mode of the horizontal alone.

The inclusive synergism illustrates the unity of phenomenological existence and communication which combines living and the lived consciousness as a person's experience of being. It is a unity of process and situation that brings the pre-conscious and conscious together as a person's consciousness. There is in this realization the unification of the immanent and transcendent dimensions of consciousness which is the interpersonal experience that inhabits a person and is shared with the other. The unity of consciousness as absence and presence constitutes the interpersonal appearance of a person and others. It is this appearing consciousness which constitutes their history. Finally, there is the unity of the pre-reflective and the reflective movement which is the simultaneous intra-personal, yet intersubjective conscious experience of people as a genetic history, that is, as inhabiting a common world.

The second conclusion as to the synoptic nature of the vertical modality manifests the person as a subjectivity from an inter-personal point of view, yet as just a person whose intra-personal nature is not divisible into subjective and objective dimensions. The vertical style of being for the person is the unity of the living, the pre-conscious, the immanent, the absence, and the prereflective consciousness experienced in silence, synchronic language and speaking. On the other hand, the synopsis of the horizontal modality points to the third conclusion that the person is an objectivity from the interpersonal perspective, yet not distinguishable as such from the intra-personal point of view. Such an objectivity is the unity of the lived, the conscious, the transcendent, the presence, and the reflective consciousness experienced in thought, diachronic language, and the speech act.

Yet, the synergism of the synoptic elements as noted thus far is only a unity, only the passive dimension of the vertical and horizontal experience that is properly phenomenological existence as being there and then. The dialectic completion of the synergism is its reversibility which I have called 'communication.' The synergism as reversibility indicates the constant exchange and encounter of the intra-personal and inter-personal modes of existence which yield perception and expression as styles of each other. This reversibility allows the dialectic integration and completion of perception as silence and thought; the constitution of expression which is synchronic and diachronic language enveloping each other; and, the genetic fulfillment of communication as such in speaking and the speech act. This dialectic critique indicates, finally, that the unity and reversibility that constitute the original ambiguity of existing are the product of consciousness and experience as the completion, yet the ground of each other. Consciousness as the genetic unity — and experience as the constitutive reversibility of the vertical and horizontal modalities — discloses the *person* as the origin and history of the perceiving-perception, the expressing-expression, and the communicating-communication. How then do words relate to the world? Words are the articulated embodiment of the person and his lived-reality.

APPENDIX

MERLEAU-PONTY'S PHENOMENOLOGY OF COMMUNICATION*

During his inaugural lecture on January 15, 1953 at the Collège de France Maurice Merleau-Ponty asserted that "the more energetic our intention to see the things themselves, the more the appearances by which they are expressed and the words by which we express them will be interposed between the things and us."[1] With this remark Merleau-Ponty emphasizes the philosophic concern with language in its modalities of expression and perception. It is a major theme of those French philosophers of the Paris School of Existentialism who have developed projects beyond the pioneering work of the founder of modern phenomenology, Edmund Husserl.

In particular, Merleau-Ponty's philosophic regard for language and reality as existential styles of expression and perception is a central issue in his phenomenology. His original and provocative philosophy emerges in a process which turns the freedom of phenomenological method, that is, description, reduction, and intentionality, to the service of existential ontology in a rigorous attempt to locate meaning as the human situation. This is to say, Merleau-Ponty presents the process nature of personal and interpersonal *Being* by examining the lived-encounters of perceptive and expressive *signs* that are experienced as communication. As Merleau-Ponty puts it, "the recognition of phenomena, then, implies a theory of reflection and a *new cogito*."[2]

In this paper I wish to suggest that Merleau-Ponty's original and distinct formulation of phenomenology is a semiotic system or synergic theory of signs founded on an interplay of : (1) The recognition of the *presence* of phenomena by description, that is, a "primacy of perception;" (2) The reflective location of meaning by structural reduction, that is, a "primordial expression;" and (3) The new *cogito* of intentionality or lived-experience in which one recognizes the "I am able to", the "I can" rather than the Cartesian formula the "I think," the "I feel."

* This paper was presented to the New Mexico and West Texas Philosophical Society at its annual meeting in May 1970 at El Paso, Texas; *Philisophy Today*, 14, no. 2 (Summer, 1970): 79-88.

[1] Maurice Merleau-Ponty, *In Praise of Philosophy*, trans. John Wild and James M. Edie (Evanston, Illinois : Nortwestern University Press, 1963), p. 20.

[2] Maurice Merleau-Ponty, *Phenomenology of Perception*, trans. Colin Smith (New York : Humanities Press, 1962), p. 50.

In short, I want to argue that Merleau-Ponty's theory of communication or theory of intercorporeal Being is the precise formulation of a semiotic phenomenology of human existence-as-lived. In this sense Merleau-Ponty correctly hypostatizes that "each philosophy is also an architecture of signs. It constitutes itself in close relation with other modes of exchange which make up our historical and social life."[3] Hence, the immediate task is to examine respectively the modes of semiotic exchange that are perception and expression : (1) The Primacy of Perception as Method; (2) Expression as the Primordiality of Being; and (3), Semiology as a Phenomenology of Communication.

THE PRIMACY OF PERCEPTION AS METHOD

Merleau-Ponty regularly defines phenomenology as the study of essences. And as has previously been noted, the study consists in the description, reduction, and intentionality of phenomena to determine respectively content, structure, and existential meaning-as-lived. "But this also means," as Merleau-Ponty states, "that one does not go beyond the world except by entering into it and that the spirit makes use of the world, time, speech, and history in a single movement and animates them with a meaning which is never used up. It would be the function of philosophy, then, to record this passage of meaning rather than to take it as an accomplished fact."[4]

In the case of human communication, Merleau-Ponty's phenomenology concerns itself with the essences or signs of personal perception and expression which combine acts of consciousness and sensitive awareness into public encounters. Such public encounters become fixed as personal and intersubjective history. This is to say, essences are signs reflecting and constituting meaning-as-lived. Put another way, communication among people is a holistic system of signs moving through the synergism of individual perception and expression toward a state of equilibrium which is personal or shared meaning. Thus, Merleau-Ponty's phenomenology requires a study of the essence of communication, that is, a study of signs, as three progressive, yet simultaneous steps of reflection.

According to Merleau-Ponty one is first required to engage in the phenomenological description of the communication act as the propagation and reception of signs-as-meaningful. This initial analysis of the simultaneity of expression and perception requires a fundamental understanding of the personal experience of self, human embodiment. The consciousness of embodiment is precisely an awareness and understanding of the unitary *presence* of mind and body *living* in the acts of expression and perception that are the synoptic acts of *doing* that create *speaking* and *silence*. The human person or Body-subject (an unhyphenated existence!) achieves intersubjectivity or communication because he lives the simultaneous separation and union of perception and expression *in* himself and *with* others. This is to suggest that I think and I feel or I conceive and I sense, but such a separation and union

[3] Merleau-Ponty, *In Praise of Philosophy*, p. 57.
[4] Ibid., p. 9.

of mind and body is descriptive only of *living*. Living is a synoptic whole greater than the sum of its parts and not divisible into its parts. As Merleau-Ponty formulates this idea, "in order to be themselves, freedom and spirit must witness themselves in matter or in the body; that is to say, they must express themselves."[5]

In the descriptive process of specifying the signs which constitute the communication *Gestalt*, there is a "primacy of perception" for Merleau-Ponty. The content of communication is experienced as a *perception of*, a *consciousness of* what is expressed by oneself or others. The phenomena of perception allow one to "see" the essential modality or so-called "objectivity" of lived-experience which is communicated. The descriptive procedure allows the Body-subject to be conscious of the reality that is lived in the many acts of personal becoming. That is, meaning takes on reality by functioning as an orientation in a person's life-world (*Lebenswelt*). Each person comes to discover and recognize his Body-subject as an instrument of the ability to act, the ability to live authentically. Thus, the human personality senses and knows the direction of his very Being as he arrives at the threshold of an intentional-object. In short, phenomena become meaningful when experienced-as-lived, experienced-as-signs, rather than as conceived, as sensed symbols.

Description, then, captures and encloses the meaning present in the consciousness of myself and others which constitutes a shared history of inhabitants. As Merleau-Ponty explains, the "communicative life of men" is history in the existential sense of human *immanence*.[6] Description in the phenomenological sense is precisely the location of immanent signs which are expressively and perceptively co-present in lived-behavior.

The second step in philosophic analysis for Merleau-Ponty is a "radical reduction" or the specification of the structure of phenomena, in a phrase, the phenomenological reduction of the essential *Gestalt*. The process is "radical" because it is synergic rather than synthetic in the Hegelian sense. The structural estimation of personal lived-experience is descriptive of both self-realization and the empathy acknowledged in relations with other people. For example, a speaker encounters the structure of communication when he is conscious of the meaning which a listener infers precisely when that listener's response or lack of response is also determinate of the speaker's perception of his own expression, and indeed, perception of his ability to further engage the communicative act. As Merleau-Ponty concisely states, "to the extent that what I say has meaning, I am a different 'other' for myself when I am speaking; and to the extent that I understand, I no longer know who is speaking and who is listening."[7]

Yet, one must go beyond the superficial designation of essential structural relations to the existential structure of meaning. That is, one must "bracket" his experience as a conscious act. By bracketing one engages in the process of analysis devoid of the influence of personal lived-experience as an "ob-

[5] Ibid., pp. 29-28.

[6] Ibid., p. 11.

[7] Maurice Merleau-Ponty, *Signs*, trans. Richard C. McCleary (Evanston, Illinois : Northwestern University Press, 1964), p. 97.

jective" orientation. In particular, the investigator should suspend his analytic, philosophic, sensual and other prejudices or predispositions as to the nature of perception or the phenomena to be perceived. With the completion or bracketing — as far as it be possible — one is able to recognize the essential structures of phenomena as reductive to existential phenomena. For example, one witnesses and engages in private behavior which is universal to one's interpersonal experience with others, as opposed to situationally dependent behavior.

At this level of inquiry meaning emerges as a structural unit independent of affective or rationalized content borne by a person or his situation. Put another way, the transcendent signs of phenomena compare and contrast with immanent signs thus specifying the phenomenal presence. What is essentially given as signified unites with what is transcendentally given as signifying; thus emerges meaningful, significant phenomena. This is by way of saying that the phenomenological reduction allows an experiential structure to become knowable as the existential fiber or style in a person's lived-experience. Indeed, one comes to the genesis of meaning which is the sign-to-signification; it is the "sedimentation" of personal experience into intersubjectivity.

If one fails to bracket his perspective inquiry, an inability to distinguish *structure* and the *consciousness of structure* arises, where in fact the consciousness of structure functions as a content for structure, an "objectivity". Consequently, structure (the existential) is perceived incorrectly as a sole function of content (the essential). In other words, the phenomenological reduction involves the suspension of the consciousness of phenomenal content (sign-to-signification) and the realization of the phenomenal structure that is the pre-conscious (sign-as-signification) or existential meaning. This process method of perception links the immanent phenomena of description to the transcendent phenomena of reduction to discover or create a presence that is existential *per se*. The process can be exemplified in one's everyday experience of awakening from sleep.

One wakes up, so to speak, by progressing in perceptive awareness, with varying degrees of meshing, from (1) corporeal awareness of self to (2) mental or conscious recognition of self to (3) the actual synergic point where one is fully aware of his lived-behavior as a unitary body-mind (Body-subject) *ability to act* in fulfillment of pre-conscious capabilities. Capabilities that are not merely physical or mental, but both. One is alive, not merely breathing or thinking.

In the brief period before one is fully aware of being awake, there is the beginning of a conscious awareness of how things really are — prior to any conceptualization, cognition or affection about the things "being as they should be." One in point of fact is perceiving the content of the phenomena around him prior to his consciousness of it, that is, prior to the structuring or designating of phenomena as meaningful. There is an existential, lived-meaning to phenomena before they are named as essential, as "objective". In short, the sign meaning is *a priori* to the act of signification.

The third and final step in Merleau-Ponty's phenomenological method is the "radical *cogito*" or *intentionality*. At this juncture Merleau-Ponty directly moves his phenomenology to an existential project. For, one is now concerned with pure intentionality devoid of consciousness and absent from the structural phenomena that are hide-bound to the pre-conscious as sign-to-signification. This is to suggest that one progresses beyond bracketed experience or "operative intentionality" which marks the first and second phase of phenomenological inquiry, that is, description and reduction. In the third step one arrives at the process of "thetic intentionality."

Thetic intentionality means the lived-experience or act of perception that contains meaning precisely because it is not dependent on the calculated maneuver of the bracketing experience; one transcends his "consciousness of" phenomena to the phenomena themselves. Thetic intentionality or existential meaning is the preconscious perception of self prior to interpersonal perception which is communication. As Merleau-Ponty says, "for the speaking subject, to express is to become aware of; he does not just express for others, but also to know himself what he intends."[8] Existential meaning is the knowledge base from which "I" realize that "I am able to" or "I can" perceive and express, as opposed to the bracketed or essential meaning in which "I think that" and "I sense that" perception and expression are engaged. In brief, bracketed experience is operative intentionality at the empirical level (a history of phenomena), while thetic intentionality is existential experience (primordial phenomena). Consequently, the existential creates the essential in the process of perception. Indeed, says Merleau-Ponty, "the philosopher is the man who wakes up and speaks."[9]

Merleau-Ponty's phenomenological method is in fact the very process of perception. This is to say, perception is marshalled to determining the essential *constructa* of experienced phenomena as a key to interpreting existential meaning. The counterpart to perception is, of course, expression and in this conjunctive role expression is the phenomena of perception. The expression of factual knowledge presents a ready-made, lived-structure of meaning (signification) in the language used (signs). By applying phenomenological techniques to articulated language (speaking), one arrives at an understanding of the semiotic meaning force of communication acts. Merleau-Ponty summarizes it well, "what we have now understood is that symbolic matrices, a language of self to self, systems of equivalences built up by the past, effect groupings, abbreviations, and distortions in a simple act and which analysis reconstitutes more and more closely."[10]

EXPRESSION AS THE
PRIMORDIALITY OF BEING

An examination of the levels of expression helps to further clarify distinctions promoted by a phenomenological method. Expression at the level of descriptions, according to Merleay-Ponty, should be designated as language (*le langage*).

---

[8] Ibid., p. 90.

[9] Merleau-Ponty, *In Praise of Philosophy*, p. 63.

[10] Maurice Merleau-Ponty, "Phenomenology and Psychonanalysis, *Preface* to Hesnard's *L'Oeuvre de Freud*" in *The Essential Writings of Merleau-Ponty*, ed. Alden L. Fisher (New York : Harcourt, Brace and World, Inc., 1969), p. 83.

At this initial stage of communication analysis Merleau-Ponty follows the explanation of the linguist Ferdinand de Saussure and defines language as the synoptic presentation of two structural sub-units which compose any given word in relation to other contextural signs (verbal and non-verbal), namely, the *signifier* and the *signified*. The signifier means simply the sound-image of a word, while the signified is the concept as implied or as understood. Thus, one narrows down a given communication act to the ordinary language (*la langue*) used and within that utterance the distinct words articulated which are identifiable by the holistic sound-image and concept. Yet, such a description still leaves the analyst far short of determining the *intended* meaning of a message. In short, linguistic structure is a behavioral factor of linguistic content as perceived, not an expressed structure of lived-experience.

The investigator should move to the second phase of inquiry by bracketing his perceptive experience of the language used in the message. Language should be approached in its neutral structural sense, much as one might attempt to do in defining a new word for a young child : unadorned structure to be filled in by lived-experience. Here language emerges as a structure devoid of historic content, that is, removed from the public situation in which it is uttered and re-uttered. Bracketed language and its meaning are what might be called *cultural* or *social significations*. The French use the word *la langue* (roughly meaning a society's current spoken tongue) as opposed to *le langage* (a symbol code and grammar) to get at this distinction. In terms of meaning analysis, a crude American equivalent might be the denotative or consensus meaning of language as opposed to the connotative or personal meaning. In any event, the task is to find the language structure implicit in a tongue or cultural signification. As Merleau-Ponty suggests, "expression presupposes someone who expresses, a truth which he expresses, and others before whom he expresses himself. The postulate of expression and of philosophy is that it can simultaneously satisfy these three conditions."[11] Once the meaning, as a hermeneutic of the *Weltanschauung*, of a message is ascertained at the structural level, one can move to the third area of phenomenological analysis. That is, one can examine intentionality in meaning which is the penetration of the lived-experience (*Lebenswelt*).

Merleau-Ponty argues that the act of speaking (*la parole*) is at the core of the "radical *cogito*." He stresses the primordiality of embodiment in communication. As he says, "expression is a matter of reorganizing things-said, affecting them with a new index of curvature, and bending them to a certain enhancement of meaning." That is "speaking to others (or to myself), I do not speak *of* my thoughts; I *speak them*, and what is between them — my afterthoughts and underthoughts."[12] For example, when one speaks there is an expression which is at the preconscious level of the speaker at the moment the words are uttered and thus rendered perceptible to myself and other conscious Body-subjects. One might readily object that he thinks before he speaks and hence is conscious of his words". This objection can be granted, not as existential speech (sign-as-significations), but as a description

[11] Merleau-Ponty, *In Praise of Philosophy*, p. 30.
[12] Merleau-Ponty, *Signs*, p. 19.

of bracketed speech or the use of a cultural meaning, an "objectivity" of sign-to-signification. When the conscious, rational scrutiny of language is absent, for example in the impromptu speech, one is speaking at the existential level or pre-conscious level of expression. There is in the impromptu speech experience an awareness of personal communication with self and others through language and body which is the felt or lived-awareness of primordial self-expression — a fact exploited by the psychologist in the verbal technique of "free association."

One can therefore express himself at the level of existential awareness that is properly preconscious and revealing of one's private reality. Being, in the metaphysical sense, is recognizeable in expression as the human structure of verbal and non-verbal behavior that is embodied, lived-intentionality. In the existential modality of expression a personal act of communication can indeed reveal one's "real" self at the interpersonal level of perception. Speaking is an existential risk, for "at the moment of expression the other to whom I address myself and I who express myself are incontestably linked together."[13] Our great care (or the lack of it!) in the use of language before other people is demonstration enough of this point.

Merleau-Ponty indicates the primordiality of being entailed by expression in his definition of speech. "Speech, as distinguished from language, is that moment when the significative intention (still silent and wholly act) proves itself capable of incorporating itself into my culture and the culture of others — of shaping me and others by transforming the meaning of cultural instruments."[14] This is to say, *speaking* displays a pre-conscious structure of private, existential meaning that becomes frozen by its verbalization — frozen into a cultural pattern that is the tongue we speak and the reality we inhabit. The interpersonal perception of existential expression (primordial signs) sediments into empirical speech (empirical signs) allowing its reuse by anyone. Thus, speech, removed from its value or social context of private or public lived-experience is mere language; it is a symbol code barren of any personal awareness in the absence of human utterance and social perception. This is precisely the distinction between the *word in the speaking* and the *spoken word.*[15]

SEMIOLOGY AS A
PHENOMENOLOGY OF COMMUNICATION

Having examined the parallel structure of perception and expression as reflected in communication analysis, an explanation of the semiotic system or sign theory underlying Merleau-Ponty's existential-phenomenological method is particularly relevant. He uses an explicit system of signs to explain both the lived-experience of perception and expression. Again emulating de Saussure, Merleau-Ponty argues that meaning is a product of the conjunction of signs. It is the synergic connection of signs, not the individual sign, that produces meaning. Even in the case where there is a void or "chasm" one en-

[13] Ibid., p. 73.
[14] Ibid., p. 92.
[15] Merleau-Ponty, *Phenomenology of Perception*, p. 197.

counters meaning, for the specific absence of a sign is also a sign to be linked to other signs. For example, the force of speaking derives in part from silence — meaning is the conjunction of what is said and what is not said.

Put another way, the occurrence of meaning is not a sign-to-signification structure, but a sign structure in which the signs *are* the signification. The existential signs are by structure primordial and self definitive, whereas empirical signs are historical and definitive only in the congruence of structure with usage content. Existential meaning consists of signs in which signifiers and signifieds (sound-image and concept in expression, or, immanent and transcendent perspective in perception) are synergic and inseparable : the sign is the signification. Meaning is the same as expressed and perceived at either the intrapersonal level or the intersubjective level. In contrast, empirical meaning consists of signs in which the signifier or immanent perception is variously joined synthetically (not synergically) to an intended signified or transcendent perception respectively. Thus, empirical expression or perception is a sign-to-signification structure where meaning as semiotic structure depends on semiotic content.[16]

The encompassing *Gestalt* nature of the semiotic process can be illustrated with two visual examples. Empirical signs are observed in the perception of a painting where the foreground is apparent in comparison with the background precisely because the perceived plane of the background is itself devoid of a "foreground." Similarly, the plane of the foreground is clearly perceptible with its equally lacking "background." The two planes join synthetically to posit one foreground and one background; the structure (signs) is a function of its content (significations). On the other hand, existential signs are equally obvious in most socalled optical illusions where foreground and background as sign structures on *one* plane are identical and thus erratically reverse themselves to the observer's consternation in attempting to focus his perspective on *two* planes. Here content must be a function of structure, for content is structure — the signs are the significations. In the "illusion" one is a constant witness to the birth of a visual object.

In both perception and expression several semiotic relations operate at the verbal and non-verbal levels of communication. The most common system is of course linguistic semiology which provides a structural model for multi-level perception and expression in a given communication analysis. Thus, speaking is semiotically divisible into language as immanently and transcendentally *expressed* or as immanently and transcendentally *perceived*. In this sense, Merleau-Ponty correctly asserts that "all perception, all action which presupposes it, and in short every human use of the body is already *primordial expression*."[17]

To explain briefly, immanent language is both expressed and perceived as a "tongue" or cultural-social signification. This is the level of empirical speech and meaning. On the other hand, transcendent language is speaking (*la parole*) in the existential sense of language which creates personal, lived-

---

[16] For example, see my "Rhetorical Criticism : An Interpretation of Maurice Merleau-Ponty," *Philosophy and Rhetoric*, II, no. 2 (Spring, 1969), pp. 61-71.

[17] Merleau-Ponty, *Signs*, p. 67.

experience. By a process of historical approval, disapproval, or modification certain existential expressions or perceptions become sedimented. They assume a public meaning content which can be used over and over again as an immanent sign structure for personal content meaning. In short, transcendent signs become sedimented into one or two possible immanent signs, that is, only one or two possible significations-for-signs.

For example, immanent signs in expression form a sediment or cultural meaning which allows communication at an empirical level. However, a speaker in his use of communication elements (language, voice, gesture, etc.) can express transcendent signs that form an existential meaning not dependent on empirical meanings. Indeed, the language which is eloquent to our ears is of this order. Yet, such existential speech may well sediment to affirm, alter, or replace empirical speech at the personal or social level. A similar structure of signs exists in the act of perception. The cultural orientation to given perspectives is on the level of empirical perception. An original and existential perception that transcends the empirical can still occur. Such a perception is generally classified as an "insight." Indeed, how many such existential "insights" are now sedimented as "accepted" or even as the "only way" of doing and saying things? Wise sayings and epigrams are exemplary of this perceptual phenomenon.

By way of caution, one should note that the immanent and transcendent elements of Merleau-Ponty's semiology are reversible at the interpersonal level when expression and perception constitute intersubjective communication. This is to say, for example, that one's personal articulations using language considered to be immanent may be perceived by another as transcendent for various reasons. Similarly, a speaker uttering existential or transcendent speech may be perceived as using empirical speech. The point to be made is that the proper understanding of the synergic union of perception and expression as a single agency can be achieved only by a phenomenological analysis of communication acts based on a semiotic division of elements.[18]

Interpersonal structures must lead back to personal structures when perception and expression are explored for their meaning, whether at the empirical or the existential level. Yet, an existential-phenomenological examination of communication is by definition limited to finding the meaning present in the elements of lived-experience which is strictly speaking a subjectivity born of intersubjectivity.[19] To separate the intrapersonal from the interpersonal in the hermeneutic analysis of perception and expression is to deny the possibility of a phenomenological reduction to the existential. On the contrary, meaning is a determinate lived-experience manifest in the communication act.

[18] This is shown in my "Speaking and Semiology : Maurice Merleau-Ponty's Phenomenological Theory of Existential Communication" (unpublished Ph. D. dissertation, Dept. of Speech, Southern Illinois University, 1969), pp. 1-423.

[19] See James L. Bemis and Gerald M. Phillips," A Phenomenological Approach to Communication Theory," *Speech Teacher*, XIII, no. 4 (November, 1964), pp. 262-269; and, Richard B. Gregg, "A Phenomenologically Oriented Approach to Rhetorical Criticism," *Central States Speech Journal*, XVII (May, 1966), pp. 83-90.

CONCLUSIONS

Several conclusions can now be drawn from the present analysis of Merleau-Ponty's semiotic phenomenology.

1. Communication is a synergic process of perception and expression which is both intrapersonal and interpersonal.

2. Communication is a synergic process (a) of empirical and existential speech, and (b) of immanent and transcendent perception.

3. Existential-phenomenological analysis utilizes a semiotic system to distinguish empirical and existential modes of perception and expression.

4. The semiotic integration of description, reduction, and intentionality allows for an existential hermeneutic of communication acts.

By way of final comment, one should note that Merleau-Ponty's existential-phenomenological approach to communication analysis is by definition a project in intersubjective semiotics as a function of personal expression and perception. It is a philosophic approach that utilizes the semiotic model as a paradigm for an approach to locating meaning in personal and public encounters with Being and Reality. As Merleau-Ponty remarks, "in a sense, the highest point of philosophy is perhaps no more than rediscovering these truisms : thought thinks, speech speaks, the glance glances. But each time between the two identical words there is the whole spread one straddles in order to think, speak, and see."[20]

---

[20] Merleau-Ponty, *Signs*, p. 21.

BIBLIOGRAPHY

1. BOOKS

ALEXANDER, HUBERT G. *The Language and Logic of Philosophy.* Albuquerque : University of New Mexico Press, 1972.

—, *Meaning in Language.* Glenview, Illinois : Scott, Foresman and Co., 1969.

ALSTON, WILLIAM P., *Philosophy of Language.* Englewood Cliffs, New Jersey : Prentice-Hall, Inc., 1964.

AUGENSTEIN, L. G., *Communication : A Discussion at the Nobel Conference.* Amsterdam and London : North-Holland Publishing Co., 1969.

AUSTIN, JOHN L., *How to Do Things with Words.* Edited by J. O. Urmson. New York : Oxford University Press, 1968.

—, *Philosophical Papers.* Edited by J. O. Urmson and G. J. Warnock, 2nd ed. London : Oxford University Press, 1970.

AYER, A. J., *Metaphysics and Common Sense.* London : Macmillan and Co., Ltd., 1969.

AYER, A. J., *et al., Studies in Communication.* London : Martin Secker and Warburg, 1955.

BAIRD, A. CRAIG, *Rhetoric : A Philosophical Inquiry.* New York : The Ronald Press Co., 1965.

BERLIN, SIR ISAIAH, *et al., Essays on J. L. Austin.* Oxford : At the Clarendon Press, 1973.

BITZER, LLOYD F., and BLACK, EDWIN, eds., *The Prospect of Rhetoric.* Englewood Cliffs, New Jersey : Prentice-Hall, Inc., 1971.

CARE, N. S., and LANDESMAN, C., eds. *Readings in the Theory of Action.* Bloomington and London : Indiana University Press. 1968.

CATON, CHARLES E., ed. *Philosophy and Ordinary Language.* Urbana : University of Illinois Press, 1963.

CHAPPEL, V. C., ed. *Ordinary Language.* Englewood Cliffs, New Jersey : Prentice-Hall, Inc., 1964.

CHOMSKY, NOAM, *Aspects of the Theory of Syntax.* Cambridge : The M.I.T. Press, 1965.

DANCE, FRANK E. X., ed. *Human Communication Theory* : *Original Essays.* New York : Holt, Rinehart, and Winston, Inc., 1967.

DOUGLAS, DONALD G., ed. *Philosophers on Rhetoric* : *Traditional and Emerging Views.* Skokie, Illinois : National Textbook Co., 1973.

FANN, K. T., ed. *Symposium on J. L. Austin.* London : Routledge and Kegan Paul, 1969.

FEIGL, H., and SELLARS, W., eds. *Readings in Philosophical Analysis.* New York : Appleton-Century-Crofts, 1949.

FLEW, ANTONY, ed. *Essays in Conceptual Analysis.* New York : St. Martin's Press, 1966.

—, *Logic and Language.* First and Second Series. Garden City, New York : Doubleday and Co., Inc., 1965.

FODOR, J. A., and KATZ, J. J., eds. *The Structure of Language.* Englewood Cliffs, New Jersey : Prentice-Hall, Inc., 1964.

FURBERG, MATS, *Saying and Meaning* : *A Main Theme in J. L. Austin's Philosophy.* Oxford : Basil Blackwell, 1971.

GANZ, JOAN SAFRAN, *Rules* : *A Systematic Study.* The Hague and Paris : Mouton and Co., 1971.

GARDINER, SIR ALAN HENDERSON, *The Theory of Speech and Language.* Oxford : At the Clarendon Press, 1951.

GEACH, P. T., *Reference and Generality.* Ithaca, New York : Cornell University Press, 1962.

GOODMAN, NELSON, *Languages of Art* : *An Approach to a Theory of Symbols.* London : Oxford University Press, 1969.

GOTTLIEB, G., *The Logic of Choice* : *An Investigation of the Concept of Rule and Rationality.* New York : Macmillan, 1968.

HARE, R. M., *Freedom and Reason.* London : Oxford University Press, 1963.

—, *The Language of Morals.* New York : Oxford University Press, 1968.

HEIDEGGER, MARTIN, *Being and Time.* Trans. John Macquarrie and Edward Robinson. New York : Harper and Row, Publishers, 1962.

HOOK, SIDNEY, ed. *Language and Philosophy.* New York : New York University Press, 1969.

KANT, IMMANUEL, *Critique of Pure Reason.* Edited by Norman Kemp Smith. New York : St. Martin's Press, 1929. First published in 1781.

KATZ, JERROLD J., *The Philosophy of Language.* New York : Harper and Row, 1966.

—, *The Underlying Reality of Language and Its Philosophical Import.* New-York : Harper Torchbooks, 1971.

LANDESMAN, CHARLES, *Discourse and Its Presuppositions.* New Haven and London : Yale University Press, 1972.

LANIGAN, RICHARD L., *Speaking and Semiology* : *Maurice Merleau-Ponty's Phenomenological Theory of Existential Communication.* The Hague and Paris : Mouton and Co., 1972.

LEWIS, DAVID K., *Convention* : *A Philosophical Study.* Cambridge : Harvard University Press, 1969.

LINSKY, LEONARD, ed. *Semantics and the Philosophy of Language.* Urbana : University of Illinois Press, 1952.

LOCKE, JOHN, *An Essay Concerning Human Understanding.* 2 vols. New York : Dutton, 1961.

LYONS, JOHN, *Introduction to Theoretical Linguistics.* Cambridge : At the University Press, 1969.

MACE, C. A., ed. *British Philosophy in Mid-Century* : *A Cambridge Symposium.* 2nd ed. London : George Allen and Unwin, Ltd., 1966.

MERLEAU-PONTY, MAURICE, *Consciousness and the Acquisition of Language.* Trans. by Hugh J. Silverman. Evanston, Illinois : Northwestern University Press, 1973.

—, *Phenomenology of Perception.* Trans. by Colin Smith. London : Routledge and Kegan Paul, 1962.

—, *In Praise of Philosophy.* Trans. by John Wild and James Edie. Evanston, Illinois : Northwestern University Press, 1963.

MINNIS, NOEL, ed. *Linguistics at Large.* London : Victor Gollancz, Ltd., 1971.

MISCHEL, THEODORE, ed. *Human Action.* New York : Wiley, 1969.

NATANSON, MAURICE, and JOHNSTONE, JR., HENRY W., eds. *Philosophy, Rhetoric and Argumentation.* University Park : The Pennsylvania State University Press, 1965.

OLSHEWSKY, THOMAS M., ed. *Problems in the Philosophy of Language.* New York : Holt, Rinehart and Winston, 1969.

PARKINSON, G. H. R., ed. *Theory of Meaning.* London : Oxford University Press, 1968.

PASSMORE, JOHN A., *A Hundred Years of Philosophy.* Baltimore, Maryland : Penguin Books, Inc., 1968.

PERELMAN, CHAIM, and OLBRECHTS-TYTECA, L., *The New Rhetoric* : *A Treatise on Argumentation.* Notre Dame and London : University of Notre Dame Press, 1969.

PIVCEVIC, EDO, ed. *Phenomenology and Philosophical Understanding.* New York : Cambridge University Press, 1975.

QUINE, W. V. O., *From a Logical Point of View*, 2nd ed. revised, Cambridge : Harvard University Press, 1961.

—, *Word and Object.* Cambridge : The M.I.T. Press, 1964.

RHINELANDER, PHILIP H., *Is Man Incomprehensible to Man?* San Francisco : W. H. Freeman and Co., 1974.

ROLLINS, C. D., ed. *Knowledge and Experience*. Pittsburgh : University of Pittsburgh Press, 1966.

ROSENBERG, J. F., and TRAVIS, C., eds. *Readings in the Philosophy of Language*. Englewood Cliffs, New Jersey : Prentice-Hall, 1971.

RUSSELL, BERTRAND, *Logic and Knowledge* : *Essays 1901-1950*. Edited by Robert C. Marsh. London : George Allen and Unwin, Ltd., 1956.

SADOCK, JERROLD M., *Toward a Linguistic Theory of Speech Acts*, New York : Academic Press, 1974.

SCHIFFER, STEPHEN R., *Meaning*. Oxford : At the Clarendon Press, 1972.

SEARLE, JOHN R., ed. *The Philosophy of Language*. London : Oxford University Press, 1971.

—, *Speech Acts* : *An Essay in the Philosophy of Language*. Cambridge : At the University Press, 1969.

SKINNER, B. F., *Verbal Behavior*. New York : Appleton-Century-Crofts, Inc., 1957.

SPRIGGE, TIMOTHY L. S., *Facts, Words and Beliefs*. London : Routledge and Kegan Paul, 1970.

STEINBERG, D. D., and JAKOBOVITS, L. D., eds. *Semantics* : *An Interdisciplinary Reader in Philosophy, Linguistics, and Psychology*. Cambridge : At the University Press, 1971.

STEVENSON, CHARLES L., *Ethics and Language*. New Haven : Yale University Press, 1960.

STRAWSON, P. F., *Individuals* : *An Essay in Descriptive Metaphysics*. Garden City, New York : Doubleday and Co., 1963.

—, *Logico-Linguistic Papers*. London : Methuen and Co., Ltd., 1971.

—, *Philosophical Logic*. Oxford : At the University Press, 1967.

TAYLOR, DANIEL M., *Explanation and Meaning* : *An Introduction to Philosophy*. Cambridge : At the University Press, 1970.

ULLMANN, STEPHEN, *The Principles of Semantics*. Oxford : Basil Blackwell, 1957.

VENDLER, ZENO, *Linguistics in Philosophy*. Ithaca, New York : Cornell University Press, 1968.

WAISSMAN, F., *The Principles of Linguistic Philosophy*. New York. St. Martin's Press, Inc., 1968.

WALLACE, KARL R., *Understanding Discourse* : *The Speech Act and Rhetorical Action*. Baton Rouge : Louisiana State University Press, 1970.

WARNOCK, G. J., *English Philosophy Since 1900*. London : Oxford University Press, 1958.

WHATELY, RICHARD, *Elements of Rhetoric*. Edited by Douglas Ehninger and

David Potter. Carbondale, Illinois : Southern Illinois University Press, 1963. First published in 1828.

WHEATLEY, JOHN, *Language and Rules*. The Hague and Paris : Mouton and Co., 1970.

WHITE, ALAN R., *Philosophy of Action*. Oxford : At the University Press, 1971.

WILLIAMS, B., and MONTEFIORI, A., eds. *British Analytical Philosophy*. London : Routledge and Kegan Paul, 1964.

WITTGENSTEIN, LUDWIG, *The Blue and Brown Books*. New York : Harper and Row, 1965.

—, *Philosophical Investigations*. Trans. by G. E. M. Anscombe. 3rd ed. New York : The Macmillan Co., 1953.

—, *Tractatus Logico-Philosophicus*. Trans. by D. F. Pears and B. F. McGuinness. London : Routledge and Kegan Paul, 1961.

ZIFF, PAUL, *Semantic Analysis*. Ithaca, New York : Cornell University Press, 1960.

2. ESSAYS AND ARTICLES

ADAMS, E. M., "Linguistic Analysis and Epistemic Encounters." *Philosophy and Phenomenological Research* 34, no. 3 (March, 1974) : 404-414.

ALSTON, WILLIAM P., "Critical Study; (Review of) *Speech Acts : An Essay in the Philosophy of Language*, by John R. Searle." *Philosophical Quarterly* 20, no. 79 (April, 1970) : 172-179.

Encyclopedia of Philosophy, 1972 Reprint ed. S. v. "Emotive Meaning," by William P. Alston. Vol. 1-2 : 486-493.

ALSTON, WILLIAM P., "Linguistic Acts." *American Philosophical Quarterly* 1, no. 2 (April, 1964) : 138-146.

Encyclopedia of Philosophy, 1972 Reprint ed. S.v. "Meaning," by William P. Alston. Vol. 5-6 : 233-241.

ALSTON, WILLIAM P., "Meaning and Use." *Philosophical Quarterly* 13 (1963) : 107-124.

APEL, KARL-OTTO, "The A Priori of Communication and the Foundation of the Humanities." *Man and World* 5 (February, 1972) : 3-37.

ARDAL, PALL S., "And That's a Promise." *Philosophical Quarterly* 18, no. 72 (July, 1968) : 225-237.

—, "Reply to New on Promises." *Philosophical Quarterly* 19, no. 76 (July, 1969) : 260-262.

ARMSTRONG, D. M., "Meaning and Communication." *Philosophical Review* 80 (October, 1971) : 426-447.

BARKER, DONALD R., "Hypothetical Promising and John R. Searle." *Southwestern Journal of Philosophy* 3 (Winter, 1972) : 21-34.

BATES, STANLEY, "More on What We Say." *Metaphilosophy* 3 (January, 1972) : 1-24.

BEARDSWORTH, T., "Ought and Rules." *Philosophy* 45 (July, 1970) : 240-243.

BENNETT, JONATHAN, "The Meaning-Nominalist Strategy." *Foundations of Language* 10 (May, 1973) : 141-168.

BLACKBURN, S., "Searle on Descriptions." *Mind* 81 (July, 1972) : 409-414.

BRAND, MYLES, "The Language of Not Doing." *American Philosophical Quarterly* 8 (January, 1971) : 45-53.

BOYLES, JAMES E., "Language and Common Sense." *American Philosophical Quarterly* 6 (July, 1969) : 233-239.

BRUNDNZI, A. A., "Communication and Semantics." *Soviet Studies in Philosophy* 11 (Spring, 1973) : 398-410.

BURCH, ROBERT W., "Cohen, Austin and Meaning." *Ratio* 15 (June, 1973) : 117-124.

CAMERON, J. R., "'Ought' and Institutional Obligation." *Philosophy* 46, no. 178 (October, 1971) : 309-322.

—, "Sentence-Meaning and Speech Acts." *Philosophical Quarterly* 20, no. 79 (April, 1970) : 98-117.

—, "The Significance of Speech Acts and the Meaning of Words." *Philosophical Quarterly* 20, no. 79 (April, 1970) : 98-117. (Same as "Sentence-Meaning and Speech Acts".)

—, "Specification and Reference." *Philosophical Quarterly* 15, no. 58 (January, 1965) : 1-19.

—, "Specifying Versus Stating : A Reply." *Philosophical Quarterly* 19, no. 76 (July, 1969) : 255-259.

CAPPELLA, JOSEPH N., "The Functional Prerequisites of Intentional Communication Systems." *Philosophy and Rhetoric* 5 (Fall, 1972) : 231-247.

CARNAP, RUDOLF, "Empiricism, Semantics, and Ontology." *Revue Internationale de Philosophie* 4 (1950) : 20-40.

—, "Meaning and Synonymy in Natural Languages." *Philosopical Studies* 6, no. 3 (April, 1955) : 33-47.

—, "On Some Concepts of Pragmatics." *Philosophical Studies* 6, no. 6 (December, 1955) : 89-91.

CATON, HIRAM, "Speech and Writing as Artifacts." *Philosophy and Rhetoric* 2, no. 1 (Winter, 1969) : 19-36.

CAVELL, STANLEY, "Must We Mean What We Say?" *Inquiry* 1, no. 3 (Autumn, 1958) : 172-212.

CHERRY, CHRISTOPHER, "Regulative Rules and Constitutive Rules." *Philosophical Quarterly* 23, no. 93 (October, 1973) : 301-315.

CHISHOLM, RODERICK M., "A Note on Carnap's Meaning Analysis." *Philosophical Studies* 6, no. 6 (December, 1955) : 87-89.

CHOMSKY, NOAM, "Skinner's *Verbal Behavior.*" *Language* 35 (1959) : 26-58.

CLARKE, DAVID S., "Is There Meaning Independent of Force?" *Southern Journal of Philosophy* 9 (Fall, 1971) : 259-264.

CLARKE, MICHAEL, "Descriptions and Speech Acts." *Journal of Philosophy* 68 (July 1, 1971) : 400-405.

COHEN, L. J., "The Non-Existence of Illocutionary Forces : A Reply to Mr. Buch." *Ratio* 15 (June, 1973) : 125-131.

—, "Searle's Theory of Speech Acts." *Philosophical Review* 79 (October, 1970) : 545-557.

—, "Do Illocutionary Forces Exist?" *Philosophical Quarterly* 14, no. 55 (April, 1964) : 118-137.

COLE, RICHARD, and KAHANE, HOWARD, "Hard and Soft Intentionalism." *Review of Metaphysics* 23 (March, 1970) : 399-416.

COOPER, DANIEL E., "Meaning and Illocutions." *American Philosophical Quarterly* 9 (January, 1972) : 69-77.

CUSHMAN, DONALD, and WHITING, GORDON C., "An Approach to Communication Theory : Toward Consensus on Rules." *Journal of Communication* 22, no. 3 (September, 1972) : 217-238.

DAVIDSON, DONALD, "Action and Reaction." *Inquiry* 13 (Summer, 1970) : 140-148.

DOORBAR, ROGER, "Meaning, Rules and Behavior." *Mind* 80 (January, 1971): 29-40.

DOWNING, F. GERALD, "Ways of Deriving 'Ought' from 'Is'." *Philosophical Quarterly* 22 (July, 1972) : 234-247.

DUNCAN-JONES, AUSTIN, "Performance and Promise." *Philosophical Quarterly* 14, no. 55 (April, 1964) : 97-117.

FABER, RICHARD N., "Statements and What is Stated." *Philosophical Studies,* 23 (February, 1972) : 32-47.

FACIONE, PETER A., "The Problem of Defining Utter's Meaning." *Southwestern Journal of Philosophy* 3 (Winter, 1972) : 75-84.

FILLMORE, CHARLES J., "Subjects, Speakers, and Roles." *Synthese* 21 (October, 1970) : 251-274.

FODOR, JERRY, "Troubles about Actions." *Synthese* 21 (October, 1970) : 298-319.

FOTION, N., "Master Speech Acts." *Philosophical Quarterly* 21, no. 84 (July, 1971) : 233-243.

—, "Indicating Devices?" *Philosophy and Rhetoric* 8, no. 4 (Fall, 1975) : 230-237.

FREGE, GOTTLOB, "Sense and Reference (A Translation of Frege's *Ueber Sinn und Bedeutung*)." Trans. by Max Black. *Philosophical Review* 57, no. 3 (May, 1948) : 207-230.

FRIES, CHARLES C., "Meaning and Linguistic Analysis." *Language* 30, no. 1 (January-March, 1954) : 57-68.

FRIEDMAN, MAURICE, "Language and Living Speech." *Philosophy Today* 13 (Spring, 1969) : 43-47.

FRYE, MARILYN, "Force and Meaning." *Journal of Philosophy* 70 (May 24, 1973) : 281-294.

GALLAGHER, KENNETH T., "Some Recent Anglo-American Views on Perception." *International Philosophical Quarterly* 4, no. 1 (February, 1964) : 122-141.

GARNER, RICHARD T., "On Saying What is True." *Nous* 6 (Summer, 1972) : 201-223.

GEACH, P. T., "Ascriptivism." *Philosophical Review* 69 (April, 1960): 221-225.

—, "Assertion." *Philosophical Review* 74, no. 4 (October, 1965) : 449-465.

GENOVA, A. C., "Assertion and Evaluation in Searle's Theory of Speech." *Southwestern Journal of Philosophy* 2 (Spring-Summer, 1971) : 65-72.

—, "Searle's Use of 'Ought'." *Philosophical Studies* 24 (May, 1973) : 183-191.

GILL, JERRY H., "Linguistic Phenomenology." *International Philosophical Quarterly* 13, no. 4 (December, 1973) : 535-550.

GINSBERG, MITCHELL, "How to Say it and Mean it." *Philosophical Studies* 22 (April, 1971) : 43-48.

GLASGOW, W. D., "The Acts of Praising." *Theoria* 35, no. 3 (1969) : 185-203.

GOLDBERG, BRUCE, "The Linguistic Expression of Feeling." *American Philosophical Quarterly* 8 (January, 1971) : 86-92.

GRAY, BENNISON, "The Problem of Meaning in Linguistic Philosophy." *Logique et Analyse* 15 (September-December, 1972) : 609-627.

GREEN, O. H., "Intentions and Speech Acts." *Analysis* 29, no. 3 (January, 1969) : 109-112.

GREENLEE, DOUGLAS, "Why Language is not an Instrument." *Dialogue* 9 (1970) : 380-388.

GRICE, H. P., "Meaning." *Philosophical Review* 66, no. 3 (July, 1957) : 377-388.

—, "Utterer's Meaning and Intentions." *Philosophical Review* 78 (April, 1969) : 147-177.

—, "Utterer's Meaning, Sentence-Meaning, and Word-Meaning." *Foundations of Language* 4 (1968) : 1-18.

HABERMAS, JÜRGEN, "Toward a Theory of Communicative Competence." *Inquiry* 13 (Winter, 1970) : 360-3775.

HARE, R. M., "Meaning and Speech Acts." *Philosophical Review* 79 (January, 1970) : 3-24.

HARMAN, GILBERT, "Quine on Meaning and Existence, I." *Review of Metaphysics* 21, no. 1, issue no. 81 (September, 1967) : 124-151.

—, "Quine on Meaning and Existence, II." *Review of Metaphysics* 21, no. 2, issue no. 82 (December, 1967) : 343-367.

HARRIES, KARSTEN, "Wittgenstein and Heidegger : The Relationship of the Philosopher to Language." *Journal of Value Inquiry* 2 (Winter, 1968) : 281-291.

HARRIS, JAMES, "The Concept of Authority and Performative Utterances." *Southern Journal of Philosophy* 8 (Summer-Fall, 1970) : 215-222.

HARRISON, JONATHAN, "Knowing and Promising." *Mind* 71 (1962) : 443-457.

HEAL, JANE, "Explicit Performative Utterances and Statements." *Philosophical Quarterly* 24, no. 95 (April, 1974) : 106-121.

HERRING, O. F., "Cameron on Specification." *Philosophical Quarterly* 19, no. 76 (July, 1969) : 251-254.

HOLBOROW, LES C., "The Commitment Fallacy." *Nous* 5 (November, 1971) : 385-394.

HOLDCROFT, DAVID, "Meaning and Illocutionary Acts." *Ratio* 6 (1964) : 128-143.

HOUSTON, J., "Truth Valuation of Explicit Performatives." *Philosophical Quarterly* 20, no. 79 (April, 1970) : 139-149.

HUNGERLAND, ISABEL C., "Contextual Implication." *Inquiry* 3, no. 4 (Winter, 1960) : 211-258.

IMLAY, ROBERT A., "Searle on Analyticity." *Philosophical Studies* 24 (October, 1970) : 78-80.

ITKONEN, ESA, "On Grice's, Strawson's, and Searle's Concept of Meaning." *Ajatus* 34 (1972) : 149-154.

JACK, HENRY, "On the Analysis of Promises." *Journal of Philosophy* 55, no. 14 (July 3, 1958) : 597-604.

JACOBSEN, KLAUS H., "How to Make the Distinction between Constative and Performative Utterances." *Philosophical Quarterly* 21 (October, 1971) : 359-360.

KATZ, JERROLD J., "The Relevance of Linguistics to Philosophy." *Journal of Philosophy* 62, no. 20 (October 21, 1965) : 590-602.

KATZ, JERROLD J., and FODOR, JERRY A., "The Structure of a Semantic Theory." *Language* 39, no. 2, part I (April-June, 1963) : 170-210.

KING-FARLOW, JOHN, "Saying, Doing, Being, and Freedom of Speech." *Philosophy and Rhetoric* 2, no. 1 (Winter, 1969) : 37-48.

KOLENDA, KONSTANTIN, "Searle's 'Institutional Facts'." *Personalist* 53 (Spring, 1972) : 188-192.

—, "Speech Acts and Truth." *Philosophy and Rhetoric* 4 (Fall, 1971) : 230-241.

LANG, BEREL, "Space, Time, and Philosophical Style." *Critical Inquiry* 2, no. 2 (Winter, 1975) : 263-280.

LANIGAN, RICHARD L., "Aristotle's Rhetoric : Addendum to the Organon." *Dialogue* 11, no. 2 (November, 1969) : 1-6.

—, "Enthymeme : The Rhetorical Species Aristotle's Syllogism." *Southern Speech Communication Journal* 29, no. 3 (Spring, 1974) : 207-222.

—, "Maurice Merleau-Ponty Bibliography." *Man and World* 3, no. 3 (Fall, 1970) : 289-319.

—, "Merleau-Ponty, Semiology and the New Rhetoric." *Southern Speech Communication Journal* 40, no. 2 (Winter, 1975) : 127-141.

—, "Merleau-Ponty on Signs in Existential Phenomenological Communication" in *Studies in Language and Linguistics 1972-73*. Edited by Ralph W. Ewton and Jacob Ornstein. El Paso, Texas : Texas Western Press, 1972. Chapter 5 : 73-88.

—, "The Phenomenology of Speech and Linguistic Discontinuity". *Degrés : Revue de synthèse et orientation sémiologique* 1, no. 2 (April, 1973) : 1-7.

—, "Rhetorical Criticism : An Interpretation of Maurice Merleau-Ponty." *Philosophy and Rhetoric* 2, no. 2 (Spring, 1969) : 61-71.

—, "Semiotic Expression and Perception : Merleau-Ponty's Phenomenology of Communication." *Philosophy Today* 14, no. 2 (Summer, 1970) : 79-88.

—, "The 'Speech Act' Paradigm in Current Analytic Philosophy." *Speech Communication Module : Educational Resources and Information Center* selection announced in *Resources in Education* (November, 1974). (E.R.I.C. is an information retrieval system.)

—, "The Speech Act Theory of Interpersonal Communication : Stimulus for Research." *Journal of Applied Communication Research* 3, no. 2 (November, 1975) : 98-101.

—, "Two Species of Style in Aristotle." *Dialogue* 10, no. 1 (May, 1968) : 1-5.

LINDER, MICHAEL, "John R. Searle's Derivation of 'Ought' from 'Is'." *Dialogue* 14 (January, 1972) : 52-59.

LONDEY, DAVID, "On the Uses of Fact-Expressions." *Theoria* 35 (1969) : 70-79.

MACKINNON, EDWARD, "Language, Speech, and Speech-Acts." *Philosophy and Phenomenological Research* 34, no. 2 (December, 1973) : 224-238.

MARGOLIS, JOSEPH, "Meaning, Speaker's Intention, and Speech Acts." *Review of Metaphysics* 26 (June, 1973) : 681-695.

MELDIN, A. I., "On Promising." *Mind*, *N.S.* 65, no. 257 (January, 1956) : 49-66.

—, "Expressions, Descriptions, Performatives." *Philosophy and Phenomenological Research* 29, no. 4 (June, 1969) : 498-505.

MEW, PETER, "Conventions on Thin Ice." *Philosophical Quarterly* 21, no. 85 (October, 1971).

MIDGLEY, G. C. J., "Linguistic Rules." *Proceedings of the Aristotelian Society*, *N.S.* 59 (June 8, 1959) : 271-290.

MOLINE, JON, "An Approach to the Analysis of Rules." *Theoria* 35 (1969) : 168-182.

MACKAY, ALFRED F., "Professor Grice's Theory of Meaning." *Mind* 81 (January, 1972) : 57-66.

MACKINNON, EDWARD, "Language, Speech, and Speech Acts." *Philosophy and Phenomenological Research* 34 (December, 1973) : 224-238.

MCCATHY, T. A., "A Theory of Communicative Competence." *Philosophy of the Social Sciences* 3 (June, 1973) : 135-154.

MCCLOSKEY, H. J., "Two Concepts of Rules : A Note." *Philosophical Quarterly* 22, no. 89 (October, 1972).

NARVESON, JAN F., "Promising, Expecting, and Utility." *Canadian Journal of Philosophy* 1 (December, 1971) : 207-234.

NEW, C. G., "Ardal on Promises and Statements." *Philosophical Quarterly* 19, no. 75 (April, 1969) : 159-160.

NEWCOMB, THEODORE M., "An Approach to the Study of Communication Acts." *Psychological Review* 60 (November, 1963) :   393-404.

NOBLE, CLYDE E., "An Analysis of Meaning." *Psychological Review* 59, no. 6 (November, 1952) : 421-430.

NORDENSTAM, T., "On Austin's Theory of Speech-Acts." *Mind* 75 (1966).

O'NEILL, B. C., "Conventions and Illocutionary Force." *Philosophical Quarterly* 22, no. 88 (July, 1972) : 215-233.

OHMANN, RICHARD, "Speech Acts and the Definition of Literature." *Philosophy and Rhetoric* 4 (Winter, 1971) : 1-19.

OSGOOD, CHARLES E., "Studies on the Generality of Affective Meaning Systems." *American Psychologist* 17, no. 1 (January, 1962) : 10-28.

PAHEL, K. R., "Some Notes on Austin's How to do Things with Words." *Mind* 78 (July, 1969) : 433-436.

PLOCHMANN, GEORGE KIMBALL, "Metaphysical Truth and the Diversity of Systems." *Review of Metaphysics* 60 (1961) : 51-66.

POSPESEL, HOWARD, "The Nonexistence of Propositions." *Monist* 53, no. 2 (April, 1969) : 280-292.

PRZELECKI, MARIAN, and WOJCICKI, RYSZARD, "The Problem of Analyticity." *Synthese* 19 (April, 1969) : 374-399.

PUTNAM, HILARY, "Meaning and Reference." *Journal of Philosophy* 70, no. 19 (November 8, 1973) : 699-711.

QUINE, W. V., "Philosophical Progress in Language Theory." *Metaphilosophy* 1 (January, 1970) : 2-19.

RANSDELL, JOSEPH, "Constitutive Rules and Speech-Act Analysis." *Journal of Philosophy* 68 (July 1, 1971) : 385-399.

RAWLS, JOHN, "Two Concepts of Rules." *Philosophical Review* 64, no. 1, issue 369 (January, 1955) : 3-32.

REINHARDT, L. R., "Propositions and Speech Acts." *Mind* 76, no. 302 (April, 1967) : 166-183.

RICHARDS, BARRY, "Searle on Meaning and Speech Acts." *Foundations of Language* 7 (November, 1971) : 519-538.

RORTY, AMELIE C., "Belief and Self-Description." *Inquiry* 15 (Winter, 1972) : 387-410.

RUBEN, DAVID-HILLEL, "Searle on Institutional Obligation." *Monist* 56 (October, 1972) : 600-611.

RYLE, GILBERT, "Ordinary Language." *Philosophical Review* 62 (1953) : 167-186.

RYLE, GILBERT, and FINDLAY, J. N., "Use ,Usage, and Meaning." *Proceedings of the Aristotelian Society* 35 (supplement), (1961) : 223-242.

SCHLICK, MORITZ, "Meaning and Verification." *Philosophical Review* 45, no. 4 (July, 1936) : 339-369.

SCHNEEWIND, JEROME, "A Note on Promising." *Philosophical Studies* 17, no. 3 (April, 1966) : 33-35.

SCHWYZER, HUBERT, "Rules and Practices." *Philosophical Review* 78 (October, 1969) : 451-647.

SEARLE, JOHN R., "Austin on Locutionary and Illocutionary Acts." *Philosophical Review* 77 (October, 1968) : 405-474.

—, "How to Derive 'Ought' from 'Is'." *Philosophical Review* 73, no. 1 (January, 1964).

—, "Meaning and Speech Acts." *Philosophical Review* 71 (1962) : 423-432.

—, "Proper Names." *Mind* 67 (1958) : 166-173.

—, "What is a Speech Act?" in *Philosophy in America*. Edited by Max Black. Ithaca, New York : Cornell University Press, 1965.

—, "Human Communication Theory and the Philosophy of Language : Some Remarks" in *Human Communication Theory : Original Essays*. Edited by Frank E. X. Dance. New York : Holt, Rinehart, and Winston, Inc., 1967.

SEIDENSTICKER, WILLIAM D., "Language as Communication : A Criticism." *Southwestern Journal of Philosophy* 2 (Winter, 1971) : 31-39.

SELLARS, WILFRID, "Language as Thought and Communication." *Philosophy and Phenomenological Research* 29, no. 4 (June, 1969) : 506-527.

SESONSKE, ALEXANDER, "Performatives." *Journal of Philosophy* 62, no. 17 (September 9, 1965) : 459-468.

—, "Saying, Being and Freedom of Speech." *Philosophy and Rhetoric* 1, no. 1 (January, 1968) : 25-37.

SHINER, ROGER A., "Freedom of Speech-Acts." *Philosophy and Rhetoric* 3, no. 1 (Winter, 1970) : 40-50.

SHIRLEY, EDWARD S., "The Impossibility of a Speech-Act Theory of Meaning." *Philosophy and Rhetoric* 8, no. 2 (Spring, 1975) : 114-122.

SHWAYDER, D. S., "Uses of Language and Uses of Words." *Theoria* 26 (1960) : 31-43.

SINGER, MARCUS G., "The Pragmatic Use of Language and the Will to Believe." *American Philosophical Quarterly* 8 (January, 1971) : 24-34.

SKINNER, QUENTIN, "Conventions and the Understanding of Speech Acts." *Philosophical Quarterly* 20, no. 79 (April, 1970) : 118-138.

—, "On Performing and Explaining Linguistic Actions." *Philosophical Quarterly* 21 (January, 1971) : 1-21.

SLOMAN, AARON, "Transformations of Illocutionary Acts." *Analysis* 30 (December, 1969) : 56-59.

SNYDER, AARON., "Rules of Language." *Mind* 80 (April, 1971) : 161-178.

SPIEGELBERG, HERBERT, "Linguistic Phenomenology : John L. Austin and Alexander Pfänder" in *Memorias del XIII Congreso Internacional de Filosofía*. Mexico : Universidad Nacional Autonoma de Mexico, 1964.

STAAL, J. F., "Formal Logic and Natural Language : A Symposium." *Foundations of Language* 5 (May, 1969) : 256-284.

STAMPE, D. W., "Toward a Grammar of Meaning." *Philosophical Review* 77 (April, 1968) : 137-374.

STICH, STEPHEN P., "What Every Speaker Knows." *Philosophical Review* 80 (October, 1971) : 476-496.

STRAWSON, P. F., "Intention and Convention in Speech Acts." *Philosophical Review* 73, no. 4 (October, 1964) : 439-460.

—, "On Referring." *Mind* 59 (1950) : 320-344.

THAU, STEWART, "The Distinction Between Rhetic and Illocutionary Acts". *Analysis* 32 (June, 1972).

—, "Illocutionary Breakdowns." *Mind* 80 (April, 1971) : 270-275.

THOMAS, JR., SID B., "Is the Appeal to Ordinary Usage Ever Relevant in Philosophical Argument?" *Monist* 48, no. 4 (October, 1964) : 533-546.

THOMSON, JUDITH J., "Private Languages." *American Philosophical Quarterly* 1, no. 1 (January, 1964) : 20-31.

TILLMAN, FRANK, "Transcendental Phenomenology and Analytic Philosophy." *International Philosophical Quarterly* 8, no. 1 (March, 1967) : 31-40.

VUILLEMIN, J., "Expressive Statements." *Philosophy and Phenomenological Research* 29, no. 4 (June, 1969) : 485-497.

WARE, ROBERT, "Acts and Action." *Journal of Philosophy* 70, no. 13 (July 19, 1973) : 403-418.

WARNOCK, G. J., "Hare on Meaning and Speech Acts." *Philosophical Review* 80, no. 1 (January, 1971) : 80-84.

WASHELL, RICHARD F., "Towards an Ecology of Communication Forms." *Philosophy and Rhetoric* 6 (Spring, 1973) : 109-118.

WELKER, DAVID, "A Difficulty in Ziff's Theory of Meaning." *Philosophical Studies* 21 (Summer, 1970) : 54-61.

—, "Linguistic Nominalism." *Mind* 79 (October, 1970) : 569-580.

WELLS, RULON S., "De Saussure's System of Linguistics." *Word* 3, no. 1-2 (August, 1947) : 1-31.

WHITELY, C. H., "Rules of Language." *Analysis* 34 (December, 1973) : 33-38.

WILD, JOHN, "Is There a World of Ordinary Language?" *Philosophical Review* 67, no. 4 (October, 1958) : 460-476.

WILHELMSEN, FREDERICK D., "Subject Analysis in the Philosophy of Communication." *Thomist* 37 (October, 1973) : 743-761.

WILKS, Y., "Decidability and Natural Language." *Mind* 80 (October, 1971) : 497-521.

WOODRUFF, DAVID, and MCINTYRE, RONALD, "Intentionality via Intentions." *Journal of Philosophy* 68 (September 16, 1971) : 541-560.

WOODS, JOHN, "Functionality and the Logic of Relations." *Southern Journal of Philosophy* 7 (Spring, 1969) : 51-63.

ZIFF, PAUL, "On H. P. Grice's Account of Meaning." *Analysis* 28, no. 1 (October, 1967) : 1-8.

3. UNPUBLISHED MATERIALS

DIGIOVANNA, JOSEPH J., "Linguistic Phenomenology : Philosophic Method in J. L. Austin." Doctoral dissertation, Department of Philosophy, University of Notre Dame, 1972.

GLICKMANN, JACK B., "J. L. Austin's Theory of Speech Acts." Doctoral dissertation, Department of Philosophy, New York University, 1972.

LANIGAN, RICHARD L., "Existential Speech and the Phenomenology of Communication." *The Human Context/Le Domaine humain.* (Forthcoming).

—, "The Phenomenological Foundations of Semiology" in *Proceedings of the First World Congress of the International Association for Semiotic Studies—Milan, Italy, June, 1974.* The Hague and Paris : Mouton and Co., (forthcoming).

SEARLE, JOHN R., "A Classification of Illocutionary Acts." *Minnesota Studies in the Philosophy of Science*: VI., (forthcoming).

—, "Meaning, Communication, and Representation." Paper presented at the American Philosophical Association-Western Division Conference, Chicago, Illinois, April 26, 1975.

STEWART, JOHN, "Revolutionary Aspects of Austin's Speech Act Analysis." Paper presented at the Speech Communication Association Conference, Chicago, Illinois, December, 1972.

INDEX

absence, 88, 93
act, 41, 111
   communication, 25, 26, 54, 70, 77, 116
   illocutionary, 1, 8, 54ff
   locutionary, 1, 8, 41ff, 55, 56
   master speech, 75ff
   perlocutionary, 1, 8, 57, 66, 67ff
   phatic, 43, 55
   phonetic, 42, 55
   propositional, 26, 55, 60, 61ff
   rhetic, 44, 55
   rhetorical, 78ff
   speech, 41, 54, 71, 76, 77, 85, 87, 88, 102, 103ff
Adams, E.M., 82
Alexander, H.G., 9, 10
Alston, W.P., 5, 41, 47, 48
application, differential, 26
argument, 71
Aristotle, 78
art, 81
artefact, 51
ascription, 31
assertion, 31
assertives, 63
audience, 56, 77
Augenstein, L.G., 52
Austin, J.L., 1, 10, 84
Ayer, A.J., 25, 67, 69

background, 115
Baird, A.C., 78
becoming, 90
behavities, 59, 61
being, 102, 117

Bemis, J.L., 116
Berlin, I., 55
Bitzer, L.F., 80
Black, E., 80
Black, M., 39
body-subject, 109
Buber, M., 93
business, 31

Cameron, J.R., 28
Campbell, P.N., 8, 57, 68, 73
capability, 92
Care, N.S., 36
Caton, C.E., 7
Cerf, W., 84
characterization, 21
chasm, 114
Cherry, C., 40
Chomsky, N., 19, 52, 54
code, 113
cogito, 108
Cohen, L.J., 22
coherence, 18, 24
command, 22
comment, 76
commissives, 59, 60, 63
commit, 60
communicatee, 44
communication, 4ff, 10, 17, 64, 66ff, 74ff, 79, 85, 87, 102ff, 106, 117
   human, 4, 45, 57
   intention, 1, 4, 5, 23, 64
   phenomenology of, 108ff, 114ff
   principle of, 38
   theory, 4, 13, 28, 60